DENNIS TIN

D0115370

THE
COUNSEL
OF THE
UNGODLY

Faith, Hope, & Love Publishing
P.O. Box 775
Nashville, MI 49073-0775

The Counsel of the Ungodly by Dennis Tinsman

Copyright © 1994 by Dennis Tinsman. Published by Faith, Hope & Love Publishing, P.O. Box 775, Nashville, MI 49073-0775.

All Scripture quotations, unless otherwise indicated, are taken from the HOLY BIBLE, NEW INTER-NATIONAL VERSION.

Illustrations: Joseph Morrow
Editor: Suzan Otis
Cover and Book Design: Alan G. Hartman
                        TypeRight Graphics,
                        Grand Rapids, MI 49504

Library of Congress Catalog Card No.: 94-90540

ISBN 0-9643411-0-7

1 2 3 4 5 6 Printing / Year 98 97 96 95 94

Printed in the United States of America

THE COUNSEL OF THE UNGODLY

Contents

Foreword

I first met Dennis Tinsman in the worship center of Bible Baptist Church in Auburn, Washington, where I was an associate pastor. I had finished preaching a third service and was trying to sneak out the side door after speaking with a number of people when Dennis came up to me. Dennis was well dressed and presented himself well—but as we began to talk, I realized that this guy had real problems.

As usual, I struggled with selfishness and weighed in my mind whether or not it was worth getting involved with such a needy person. That evening, as I prayed about Dennis, God impressed upon me Romans 11: 5-6; "So too, at the present time there is a remnant chosen by grace. And if by grace, then it is no longer by works; if it were, grace would no longer be grace." (NIV) I had no idea that Dennis had struggled at the hands of "legalists" and "secular humanists" who had counseled him in his long journey dealing with sexual abuse as a child and his own abuse of drugs, alcohol, and himself.

Dennis and I spent many hours talking together, either on the phone, at church, or over lunches. Even though I had gone through a period of substance abuse myself, I felt totally inadequate to help Dennis with the degree of pain and abuse he had experienced. All I could do was pour as much of myself into our relationship as possible and try to point him towards the grace of God that surrounds us as freely as the air we breathe. During this time, Dennis went through some of the most painful decisions an individual can make—and yet I found Dennis to be consistently faithful, available, and teachable. Dennis grasped "grace" and did not let go.

I have just finished reading *The Counsel of the Ungodly* and can unconditionally urge you to do the same! Dennis gives a wonderfully refreshing, transparent, insider's look at the influence of secular humanism and, just as eroding to the Church, legalism and its impact upon the current counseling trends within Christianity. Dennis confronts head on the fact that we have the terrible freedom to choose sin! But he also brings to light the refreshing fact that we must be willing to accept the responsibility for our choices. From that point on, we can allow God's grace, mercy, and forgiveness to work afresh in our lives.

Through his amazing personal testimony and wonderfully told examples, you will be brought face to face with the living person of Jesus Christ and through Him, "GRACE".

At one point in Dennis' life, I was what you could call a teacher. Now I have the immeasurable privilege of being the student. Thanks, Dennis, for your ministry!

NED GRAHAM

President East Gates
Ministry International

Introduction

The apostle Paul had a past; a devastating past. Paul's memories of his past could have destroyed him emotionally and mentally. By today's diagnosis, he could have ended up with what the worldly wisdom calls a "disease". In Paul's letter to the Philippians, he expresses his victory in and through Christ to overcome his past. Philippians, chapter 3, verses 12—16 reads like this: "Not that I have already attained all this, or have already been made perfect, but I press on to take hold of that for which Christ Jesus took hold of me. Brothers, I do not consider myself yet to have taken hold of it. But one thing I do: Forgetting what is behind and straining toward what is ahead, I press on toward the goal to win the prize for which God has called me heavenward in Christ Jesus. All of us who are mature should take such a view of things. And if on some point you think differently, that too God will make clear to you. Only let us live up to what we have already attained."

"But one thing I do: Forgetting what is behind and straining toward what is ahead!" That is a tough encouragement and cannot possibly take place in anyone's life short of a miracle happening. The modern treatment for the so-called modern sin (that Satan has so elusively given different names to) has been destroying Christian people, Christian families, the Christian Church, and their testimonies for Jesus

Christ by eroding them from the inside out. Regardless of whose endorsement is on the modern treatment for the so-called modern sin, the phony labels are not scriptural and in each case have the opposite effect of that which is advertised. In a mild sense, it's like rubbing poison oak on poison ivy to relieve the poison ivy. Instead of healing, we end up with two problems. The latter is usually worse than the original.

After family, friends, and employers expelled me because I couldn't make their programs work, I decided to end it all. God's faithfulness to me remained even though I had given up on Him. I found family members, church leaders, friends, and counselors (most of whom are professing Christians) defending their worldly programs and counsel rather than the testimony of Jesus Christ. After my wife divorced me and at the completion of my first book, *A Garment of Grace*, I began to think back on all of the treatment centers, counselors, and psychiatrists whose worldly wisdom had entangled me and my loved ones. I have learned that Satan thrives on deception through desperation. He uses our love for one another to deceive us into buying into his schemes. Instead of healing, I found what I describe as "a total abomination to the grace Christ has offered us through Calvary."

The Counsel of the Ungodly is the result of 30 years of lies, double standards, perversions of grace, and hard-core legalism. I was the recipient of all of the above. The ministry of Christlike grace and compassion wasn't practiced in many of the churches I had attended. I realize now that I had been robbed of experiencing the grace that Jesus promised. Retaliation for being wronged seemed to be the standard—and measuring up to human standards, as well as people's interpretations of God's standards, dictated an impossible lifestyle for me.

After spending ten months in Michigan at a small-town church in the village of Nashville, my misconception of "worthiness" had diminished and the truth of God's grace through faith in Jesus Christ became my first love. Grace manifested itself to me as being more than a word of encouragement or part of the lyrics in a song. Grace has become a new way of life for me. The world had imposed upon me the idea that love is a two-way street. Jesus taught me through Calvary that love is not a two-way street.

By God's grace through faith in Jesus Christ, there is agape love; a love that always does what is right, no matter what the circumstances. That has become my greatest challenge. It can hurt, but it always endures. It gives and never expects anything in return; and when received, becomes the greatest gift that the Savior has ever given me to pass on.

Another word that had meaning, but was not understood by me, was perseverance. Apart from God's grace, a person cannot live out, or put into practice, Christlike perseverance. After working as an associate pastor in a Christian retirement community, I found out, from a person who has been consistent with Christ for 60 plus years, that the wisdom that comes with age is invaluable. I've learned that simplicity in Christ and trusting in Him is the only wisdom that is godly wisdom. That type of wisdom lasts an eternity. The life-saving grace of Jesus Christ . . . I'll put that up against any alternate program, treatment center, psychiatrist, psychologist, or counselor—no matter what denominational or religious title they profess to have.

The ten months I spent at that small-town church in Michigan were not continuous. After living three months in Nashville, Michigan, I returned to Federal Way—a metropolitan area south of Seattle. I began attending a church in the town of Auburn. After a semester at United Theological Seminary in Seattle, I returned to the small village of Nashville. However, while attending this church in Auburn, Washington, the foundation of grace-living that was laid in my first three months in Nashville, Michigan was being built upon in another church some 2,400 miles away. A well known evangelist's son, who was on staff there, befriended me. I couldn't imagine someone with his name taking the time and investing in what others had thrown away. My new friend told me to focus on the eternal things and leave the temporal things to God. Each time that I brought a situation to him that devastated me, he referred me to God's Word, pointed me to the cross, and told me that God loves me. The complicated walk that others had administered as a minimum requirement became obsolete and Micah, chapter 6, verse 8 became my new desire. It reads like this:

> "He has showed you, O man, what is good.
> And what does the Lord require of you?
> To act justly and to love mercy
> and to walk humbly with your God."

The Seattle area had been my home for some 25 years. I thought my divorce had eliminated me from ministry. However, my friend met with me for lunch a few days before I left to return to Michigan. I shared with him a contract from a major New York publisher that the Lord had blessed me with. He smiled and stated, "Be faithful, Dennis." I shall never forget his listening ear or the example of discipleship he portrayed. Investing in other's lives for the cause of Christ has become my new livelihood. It takes my focus off of the seemingly unsolvable problems of a devastating past and gives me a purpose in life. I have found myself drawn to other people ranging from four years old to 100 years old (literally) whose lives and situations have been tossed aside by opinionated people caught up in the rat race of everyday living. God has opened many doors. I have done very little except become available.

Two preachers—twenty years apart in age, separated by 2,400 miles, whose personalities are as different as night and day—had discipled me with more than just opinions. They pointed me to the cross, God's Word, friendship, fellowship, and mercy through their faith in Jesus Christ. I am thankful to the handful of people who have impacted my life through their faithfulness to the Savior.

After writing of the devastation and experiences, both mine and others', in the first part of *The Counsel of the Ungodly*, I reflect on "The Sunny Days". They are the good memories and the future eternity I am promised with Jesus Christ. "The Sunny Days" are the promises from God for all who believe in the Savior, as well as the biblical answer to all the ungodly wisdom. The biblical perspective of "Sunny Days" is found in Philippians, chapter 4, verse 8 and reads like this: "Finally, brothers, whatever is true, whatever is noble, whatever is right, whatever is pure, whatever is lovely, whatever is admirable—if anything is excellent or praiseworthy—think about such things." I pray that the situations, people, and grace expressed in Psalm 1 and *The Counsel of the Ungodly* touch your life or the life of someone you know with the true meaning of healing and forgiveness; a permanent healing and forgiveness that can only be found through faith in Jesus Christ.

Dedication

I wish to dedicate this book to my son,
Timothy Paul Tinsman
and my daughter,
Shannon Kristine Tinsman.

The Hands Of Grace

The smallest hands I have ever seen belonged to my son Tim. We nicknamed him Tiny Tim. Tiny was an understatement. Tim was born premature and weighed 2 pounds, 2 ounces. After a few days, his weight dropped to a startling 1 pound, 14 ounces. The prayers of many, and the grace of our Lord, would allow Tim to live and grow into a normal healthy boy. One of the fondest memories I have is of taking my pinky finger and slipping it into the grasp of his tiny, tiny hands. His little lungs couldn't breathe on their own, and I don't believe that he could have blown up a soap bubble with the volume of air his immature diaphragm produced. Although Tim needed the help of modern medicine to sustain his life and most of his body functions, the one thing he could do on his own was squeeze his daddy's finger. As the months went by, I watched those tiny, tiny hands mature and hold a bottle, a rattle, and grip the support arms on his portable wind-up swing as it moved to and fro. One year later, I watched those little hands squeeze a piece of chocolate birthday cake topped with white frosting and paint his entire face, hair, and body with the white and brown putty.

In the months that followed his first birthday, Tim would learn to fold those little hands and pray to his Lord thanking Him for his mommy, his daddy, grandma, grandpa, Brandy Bird, a pet fish named Cookie Monster, and the stuffed toys he called his buddies. Tim would express reverence before his Lord with those tiny, tiny hands. As Tim grew and grew and grew, I watched him grasp the handle bars of his bike, hold his first baseball bat, and hand me tools when I worked on the car.

The most important, significant, and eternal thing Tim ever did with his hands was to fold them in another act of reverence and ask Jesus into his heart. At 5 ½ years of age, Tim didn't understand the deep theological reasoning that Bible scholars have. He did understand, however, that he couldn't get to heaven on his mommy's or his daddy's salvation. Tim knew deep in his heart that he desired a personal relationship with Jesus Christ. Tim also knew that going to church taught him about Jesus but it was necessary for each person to ask Jesus to be their personal Savior. Tim didn't want to find himself separated from his mommy and daddy in eternity. And greatest of all, he didn't want to deny the Jesus that suffered on a cross for him.

Tim realized, at age 5 ½, that his daddy's hands were too small to hold on to for eternity. Tim's hands were growing as was the rest of him. Tim wanted to place his hands in the Savior's hands the same way his mommy and daddy had years earlier.

The most secure hands to be in are the hands of Jesus. The most miracle-filled hands that have ever existed are the hands of Jesus. Hands that once grasped straw in a stable, the sides of a wooden manger, and waved aimlessly in the presence of His virgin mother on the morning of His birth. Hands that held carpenter's tools as a young boy; hands that, as they grew older, would hold the little children; hands that made a mud pack out of saliva and dirt; hands that placed the mud pack on a blind man's eyes and gave sight to those unseeing eyes; hands that took a few loaves of bread and a small amount of fish and created a meal for five thousand people; hands that reached out to a disciple of little faith, named Peter, who lost his focus in the middle of his famous aquatic walk; hands that touched the hand of Peter's mother-in-law and took away her fever; hands that made anew the skin of a diseased leper;

hands that washed His disciples' feet; hands that served, in remembrance of Himself, the first communion; hands that folded together in a garden called Gethsemane as He humbled Himself and prayed to His heavenly father; hands that would heal a severed ear on an enemy who came to arrest Him . . . The hands of Jesus; hands that restored, hands that healed, hands that expressed the greatest love ever known to mankind when they held the sin of all in the form of two spikes driven through their flesh and bones and into a cross . . . hands that were made worthy to hold my son Tim for eternity through this miraculous act of love.

ε& ε& ε& ε& ε&

Most Gracious and Heavenly Father, thank you for the memories of Tim's little hands. Thank you for the memory of your son's hands. The hands of Jesus; hands that hold more than a memory; hands that still hold the answers to healing, restoring, cleansing, and forgiveness, until He comes again.

A Gift Of Emptiness

Like daddy like daughter? In some respects yes and in other respects, like sugar and spice and everything nice. Every daddy loves his daughter, at least this daddy does. When Shannon was born she weighed 4 pounds 4 ounces. That is exactly twice the size of her older brother, Tim, when he entered the world. I always looked at both my son and daughter as being different personalities that I loved equally. However, one character trait that Shannon had an abundance of was a sense of humor that she delivered with absolute innocence. Her daddy also has a sense of humor but it is seldom used with absolute innocence. I'll never forget one birthday a few years ago, Shannon got to her daddy's funny bone. What she did was extremely funny. The fact that she was only 4 ½ at the time made me laugh even harder. Mommy and big brother (who was almost 6 years old) literally busted a gut at the crafty and well thought out prank that was characteristic of her daddy's nature. Certainly not just any 4 ½ year old would think of manufacturing and carrying out this act of extreme humor; but Shannon did!

We all sat in a restaurant after gorging ourselves on my favorite pasttime—*Food*! As I opened my birthday gifts, I watched the expressions of excitement on Tim's and Shannon's faces. The anticipation expressed in their countenances was more enjoyable than the contents of the packages I was opening. After the customary thank yous, hugs, and kisses, something unique happened. There was still one gift that turned up unopened. No one seemed to know where it came from except for Shannon. I looked over at my wife and she appeared somewhat puzzled. Even at age six, Tim expressed total surprise and curiosity. "Open it Dad!" Shannon ordered in her excited "I can hardly wait" voice. I took the three-by-three inch package and began to unwrap it. I seemed to be more engrossed in the expressions of complete surprise in my wife's and son's faces than I did in what was inside this package. It was obvious that Shannon was the only one who knew of the surprise that would surprise everyone but her. As I completed unwrapping the package, I found another package inside. So, I unwrapped that package only to find still another package. After a few more surprises within a surprise, I finally got down to the heart of the gift—and what a gift it was! . . . . Nothing! Absolutely Nothing! We all sat still and I didn't know how to respond. My little girl was only 4 ½. I didn't want to hurt her feelings. It was obvious that she had worked very hard to make this . . . this gift of paper that wrapped a gift of absolutely nothing. I wasn't sure which layer of paper was the gift. It never dawned on me, or my wife, or Tim, that I had just fallen for the oldest trick in the book. Shannon burst out with laughter and began bouncing up and down on the padded seat of the booth where she sat. "There's nothin' there Dad!!" she shrieked. Instantly, Tim joined in with his progressive giggle that rolled back and forth to laughter and eventually turned into an extreme case of the hiccups. My wife and I both joined in the laughter with absolute astonishment at Shannon's creativity.

This prank turned into the fondest memory I have of my little girl. I remember tucking her into bed that night and thanking her for making me so happy with a gift of absolutely nothing. We even prayed together and thanked the Lord for her wonderful surprise; the surprise of emptiness.

It's hard to write about tragedy that brings forth such valuable memories to me. Two years later, Shannon's mommy divorced her daddy. The lawyer and the ungodly counsel that would drive a wedge between our family were able to take away everything except my memory, the absolute love I had for my Lord, and the grace Christ has given me to go on. I had never abused my children in any way, yet I was prevented by law from being a daddy to them. At the end of ten years of marriage, I had three suitcases of clothes, a Bible, and memories; wonderful memories. I couldn't think of anything bad Shannon had ever done. I know I had to spank her from time to time but I couldn't remember why. I suppose that's the way our Heavenly Father will view us when we get to heaven.

The grace that Jesus has given me to go on was taught to me by the Savior Himself when He cancelled my sin at the cross. I am rich with forgiveness. I even wrote a letter to Shannon's mommy's lawyer a few months after the divorce was final and told him about Jesus and the grace Christ gave me to forgive everyone, including myself.

≈ ≈ ≈ ≈ ≈

Most Gracious Heavenly Father, thank you for the memory of Shannon's gift of emptiness; a gift that made me very, very happy one birthday a few years back. Thank you also dear Lord for your gift; the gift of fullness; a fullness found in knowing, experiencing, and sharing the grace of Jesus Christ. A fullness that keeps me filled even in the times when I feel empty from the loss of my family. Thank you for your word in Colossians 2, verses 9 and 10 . . . "For in Christ all the fullness of the Deity lives in bodily form, and you have been given fullness in Christ who is the head over every power and authority."

I am thankful, Lord, that I will partake in that same fullness the generations in eternity have found because of the emptiness of a tomb on that first Easter morning some 2000 years ago.

Psalm 1

Blessed is the man
who does not walk in the counsel of the wicked
or stand in the way of sinners
or sit in the seat of mockers.
But his delight is in the law of the LORD,
and on his law he meditates day and night.
He is like a tree planted
by streams of water,
which yields its fruit in season
and whose leaf does not wither.
Whatever he does prospers.
Not so the wicked!
They are like chaff
that the wind blows away.
Therefore the wicked will not stand in the judgment,
nor sinners in the assembly of the righteous.
For the LORD watches over the way of the righteous,
but the way of the wicked will perish.

The Pebble Church

E veryone has a past or has formerly been titled something that they are not today. For instance, at one time
we were first graders and then we became second
graders and then we became third graders and so on . . .
Many of us in later years have adopted titles that start with
"ex-", referring to ourselves or others as former or previous
somethings. Take me for example. I am an ex-husband with
an ex-wife who left behind some ex-in-laws. This scenario
also makes me someone's ex-son-in-law. I no longer am
addicted to crack cocaine and alcohol, therefore, I am an ex-
drug addict and an ex-alcoholic. I have served time in
prison for armed robbery and I have been incarcerated in over
fifteen different prisons, jails, and institutions for that crime
as well as other crimes. I no longer break the law and I believe
our criminal justice system can be a necessary part of the protection, punishment, rehabilitation, and healing process. This
makes me an ex-offender and an ex-convict.

You will have to excuse me for my somewhat blunt introduction. For me, honesty has not become the best policy, it
has become the ONLY policy. You see, I've come to believe
in a book that is ten years older than eternity. It's called the
inspired Word of God. A couple of years ago, I read in this
book (known to many of us as the Bible) that the truth would
set me free—and indeed it has.

It is because of my personal relationship with Christ that I am able to rejoice in all of those "ex-'s". Without Christ, all of those "ex-'s" would stay tragedies; ugly and unresolvable issues that would cripple my life with a whole bunch of excuses and self-pity, and I'd be caught up in the never-ending web of deception and disobedience.

God is in the business of taking less-than-nothings and making somethings out of them. In the world's eyes He started with a less-than-nothing man and graciously changed me. He gave me a new life with wonderful friends, a purpose in life called ministry, and a church, a great church, a church of grace; a church filled with many formerly wounded soldiers. Yet each of those soldiers unique and very much a part of this great church.

※ ※ ※ ※ ※

I'll never forget the first time I laid eyes on it. It looked like an unbelievable work of art. Its texture was bumpy but eloquent. Its detail somewhat crude yet defined. Its shape was abstract yet right to scale. The cross on its steeple emphasized its intricate detail. The windows were transparent and even the little doors had handles on them. The roof was a miniature wooden shake type and each square on it was fitted with great patience. The name given to this beautiful work of art didn't impress me at first. The title seemed so empty. I felt a more intriguing name, a name of great splendor, would have been more appropriate. The builder named this magnificent work of art "The Pebble Church". Hundreds of little pebbles became the stone siding that gave this magnificent work of art its name as well as its splendor.

I stood there admiring it and began thinking to myself, "This is not the type of place one would expect to find a quality piece of artwork such as this." I was standing at the main security door that lead to the prison yard at the State Penitentiary in Ionia, Michigan. The showcase had many different crafts in it but none as beautiful as this. One of the prison guards approached me and asked, "See anything that catches your eye?" "Are you kidding?!" I answered back, "This church is something else!" The guard then responded with the comment, "That's an understatement." I stood there and all I could think was, "I want it!" The guard piped up again and began to inform me, "It's hard to believe almost everything used in its making came from the prison yard, including its builder. The wood chips used on the roof and the pebbles used on the sides were from the walkways. They were probably walked on for years." The guard went on to tell me with much enthusiasm, "Can you believe someone could make such a work of art out of pure garbage?"

A sense of calm settled in my spirit and the awe and wonder that had captivated my mind for a few moments gave way to new feelings; feelings of peace and feelings of extreme gratitude. I was fighting tears when I looked up at the guard and said, "I know of another church just like this one."

The text for the Bible study I was there to lead seemed to diminish from my mind and the volunteer duties I looked forward to each week began to take a back seat to new thoughts. I began to name the pebbles on the side of the church. One by one, as the faces of friends came to mind, I looked at each pebble as being unique. Their pebbly shapes began to take on the godly characteristics that I saw in each person. No two were the same but God had fitted and placed them so lovingly all around me.

I had a pebble for each and every name. In my mind, I was building this little church. I was doing in my mind what our pastor and his wife had dedicated themselves to for over thirty years. I recall Pastor telling me that he had started with eight tiny pebbles. Here I was some thirty plus years later reaping the rewards of Pastor and many other's hard work and dedication. I suppose you could say, "That's not fair." But I've not heard one pebble say that.

In any great church, we all become a part of the structure in the same way. It matters not how walked on we were or even the eloquence of our texture. It matters not how detailed our outlooks were or how defined our cultured past was or even how transparent we think we are in our faith. That tiny cross at the top of the steeple is the only qualifying mark that has allowed us to be a part of "The Pebble Church". You know, I really wanted to buy that little church but I realized that I was unable. You see, it had already been purchased by Jesus when he hung on that little cross at the top of the steeple.

CHAPTER 2

A Prison Within a Prison

The title of the seminar was "Steps to Christian Growth". The place was a high security prison with multiple barriers of various types of wire fence designed to mutilate anyone who attempted to encroach upon the exterior they protected. At strategic intervals around the perimeter were armed correction officers in towers. I had been at this correctional facility three times prior; twice as a seminar instructor and once as an "honored guest". This time, however, was different. I knew about the building at the very back corner of this multi-acre facility, but seemed to block it out of my mind during my past visits.

When I received my instructions by mail a few weeks prior to the seminar, I read over the words and ignored the punctuation which linked together the descriptive wording of my assignment. Those continuing words spelled out "Psychiatric Unit". My visits to this prison in the past as a seminar instructor had always been written out with the words "General Population" appearing after the institution's name. I guess I just ignored the specifics of my new assignment. Or perhaps the reality of it was too much. I had never turned down a seminar and over the past year I had been an instructor at approximately 15 seminars in various prisons around the state.

The thoughts of being unqualified and undereducated began to race through my mind. I had this silent fear that lingered and I tried to cover it up with an occasional joke. At any rate, I was standing in the security area wondering how to respond to a fear that was growing and seemed to penetrate deeper into every part of me.

My co-instructor was a large, stocky black man named Marcus and I just knew that the area director had mixed up our assignments. Let's get real here. Marcus was an ex-convict and had been an inmate in a high security prison years longer than I. He had also been in the prison ministry and had been a seminar instructor years longer, and had worked as a chaplain in one of the highest security prisons in the entire country a few years after his release. I felt sure that he should be the instructor at the psychiatric unit and I should resume my past responsibilities as the instructor for the general population.

Fear gripped my heart as we stood in a circle. The words of Marcus' prayer pounded through the fear. As the chaplain, Marcus, the other volunteers, and myself broke the circle and started towards the heavy steel-barred door, the fear that had subsided for a few moments was back. Three questions were dancing around in my mind: "Why this?", "Why now?", and "Why me?" You would think a man with the past I have would be "fear free". You know, the kind of label on myself similar to that of which you may find on some type of food product that reads caffeine free, fat free, cholesterol free, sugar free, and so on. The thought that big cops, ex-convicts, football players, boxers, and sumo wrestlers are fear free is a delusion.

The fear of physical harm was distant and not an issue. It wasn't a fear of failure either. This fear was one that went much deeper.

When the time came for us to part and go our separate ways, I watched as the other volunteers entered the building for the seminar with the general population. The rest of the volunteers and myself had a long walk across the prison yard to the psychiatric unit. Although this particular prison has two chaplains, it was the one assigned specifically to the psychiatric ward who joined our group.

I didn't tell the chaplain about my state of mind. I didn't want to paint a picture of unwillingness or have him think that I came unprepared. As we walked up to the large brick building, my eyes scanned the perimeter of this large facility one last time. The gun towers, wire fences, and the intimidation they have on the average everyday person, had never been minimized by me before. The posted guard opened the steel-barred door that allowed entrance to the psychiatric unit and we entered the holding area. The door shut behind us and another door of similar construction opened and I looked down a long corridor. There was a series of segregated areas in this corridor and thick wire gates set apart each of the interior units. I started repeating over and over in a silent type of whisper, "Jesus help me. Jesus help me." I now began to realize why I had this overwhelming feeling of evil.

Being genuine isn't something you try, it's something you just do. I had always been honest and empathetic in all the other seminars I had instructed. Relating to other convicts because I had been a convict brought forth some special bonding between us. Honesty and sincerity along with empathy, coupled with my absolute faith in Jesus Christ, had been the tools my Lord had used in the past to create a desire for salvation and spiritual growth in the lives of many inmates. My fear began to subside as the thoughts of how I would relate to the inmates were subdued by a transition that began to take place in my mind. I was about to face several memories that were very much a part of my past and very relevant to the fear and this present situation. As the inmates entered the dining room area, the evil sort of fear that had litcrally tried to drive me away began to leave my thoughts and an overwhelming feeling of power came over me. It was a peaceful power, a power that seemed to fill the entire room . . . and then I knew why satan had pounded so hard on me. I'm still not used to satan's sadistic, mind-captivating implantation of thoughts riddled with lies, insecurities, and immorality. There was a good reason why the devil wanted me elsewhere—and for about the next five minutes, God would show me: "Why this", "Why now", and "Why me". The peaceful thoughts of the Holy Spirit began in my head and persisted until the thoughts flowed downward and filled my heart. If the lesson had been made any clearer, I would have probably found myself in front of a burning bush with my shoes off.

I had been in other psychiatric wards since I entered the ministry. However, this was a prison within a prison and unlike any other I had ever been in. Many of the men were sedated and some were simply warehoused at this facility because society had no idea what to do with them. Being sedated made it easier for the staff to handle them. Many were kept segregated from the general population in this high security prison. In the eyes of society, I was faced with the rejected of rejects, the baddest of bad, and the hopelessness of the most hopeless.

When I say I've never been in a psychiatric ward such as this, I mean never as a man in ministry. There is a part of my life I've never really said too much about. I wanted it to become a forgotten memory; the memory of what I thought to be a very shameful situation from my past. I recall relatives years ago yelling at me when I was just a kid. In loud overbearing tones, they told me I was "a real mental case". It hurt deeply because those words, along with a very abusive childhood, bred thoughts that confused me. I suppose I had this pre-written script for my life that spelled out failure. If I recall correctly, it started when I was about eight years old. The script had been added to over the years—and by the time I enlisted in the U.S. Air Force at age seventeen, I had learned to lie my way around assuming responsibility for my actions. It was a mode I found myself in numerous times and, I believe, was a form of self-protection that became an habitual comfort zone. I would have done just about anything to get attention—including becoming a failure. Three days into boot camp, my past drug abuse, childhood dreams, and the need for individual attention found me in a mental hospital under heavy guard. The government had this sort of "debriefing" before they sent me home. I began to learn the ropes of psychological manipulation. The first morning I awoke after being heavily sedated, I met my first friend and mentor within the realm of psychotherapy. His name was A.J. He was a tall, lanky black man who was awaiting a discharge for a mental disorder. "Get up Skin-head. It's time for meds!" were A.J.'s words of introduction. "Meds" was short for medication. So I joined the rest of the men in this facility and waited in a long line to receive my issue of pills to go with breakfast. After breakfast, we sat in a circle and I listened to the other patients share their stories. When it came time for me to speak, I passed. After group therapy, A.J. pulled me aside and told me that the more problems you have, the more meds you get . . . so I invented my own little stories and stayed loaded. A.J. became an unhealthy mentor as he explained the ropes of manipulation in the not so magnificent world of psychotherapy. I adopted the name "Skin-head" from A.J. and the entire psychiatric ward thought I was an OK sort of guy. It didn't matter to me where I was as long as I was accepted. The pills were just what the devil ordered for a young man who wanted a way out. They cushioned what little conscience I had left and, instead of returning home a proud soldier, I returned home a disgrace. Once again, family members picked up where they had left off and my short tour in the Air Force became one of the highlights of unfinished responsibilities that had started when I was about eight years old and would follow me to age thirty-seven.

As the memories of the past began to fade, I realized that I indeed had brought empathy with me to this seminar titled "Steps to Christian Growth". As I looked over the men, some of whom were in their early twenties and having years to face in this prison within a prison, I opened the seminar with these

words: "Good afternoon Gentlemen. The title of this seminar is 'Steps to Christian Growth'. My name is Dennis and
this is your seminar. What you get out of it is what you put
into it. I'm an ex-convict, an ex-drug addict, and an ex-pro-
fessional liar. For some of you, you'll continue throughout this
seminar to run your games on me—and a few of you may
even fool me. You'll fool yourselves and moreover you will
even fool the highly-educated shrinks. I've been told by one
of my superiors in this ministry that I'm not here to win converts. Once again, I wish to remind you that the title of this
seminar is 'Steps to Christian Growth'. The first step in any
Christian's growth, Gentlemen, is to assume responsibility for
his actions. You can suck down the pills, make excuses for
yourselves, or let others make excuses for you. You can try to
explain your psychological profile to the courts, prosecutors,
probation and parole departments, and shift the blame and
continue to make yourselves out to be the victims. Or you
may just possibly consider—for the next two days during this
seminar—that you could possibly be responsible for your
actions and perhaps find a little honesty in all of this. At any
rate, Gentlemen, I'm gonna hang with ya' in hopes that you
will accept A New Way, A New Truth, and A New Life."

The same men that had wandered in and had looked somewhat sedated were now sitting up alert and very much
interested in what was going on.

As the seminar material was presented and the curriculum
was unfolded in front of the men, I was blessed and astound-
ed as I witnessed first hand, along with the chaplain, the birth
of honesty being manifested in the lives of the participants. I
listened as the men openly confessed their sins . . . and some
of them had been so far out of reality for so long that nothing short of a miracle would have reached them. As they
learned their Bible verses and repetitiously recited the Steps
to Christian Growth, I was blessed beyond anything I had
anticipated. I witnessed what the Gospel of Jesus Christ can
do in a life that is hopelessly, helplessly lost. I should not have

been surprised at the results of God's Word in the lives of society's rejects. After all, I was once one of those rejects. As I opened my life up to the inmates, they opened their lives up to Jesus. They wanted what I had desired for so long: Freedom! Freedom from self, freedom from the system, and freedom from sin. I continued to remind the inmates that the image they wanted to conform to wasn't my image but one that belonged to Jesus Christ—and that the Savior had graciously chosen to shine that image through me in a seminar that in the beginning I really wanted nothing to do with.

Second Corinthians, chapter 4, verses 7—10 reads like this: "But we have this treasure in jars of clay to show that this all-surpassing power is from God and not from us. We are hard pressed on every side, but not crushed; perplexed, but not in despair; persecuted, but not abandoned; struck down, but not destroyed. We always carry around in our body the death of Jesus, so that the life of Jesus may also be revealed in our body."

&a &a &a &a &a

There is more than one type of prison. Many of us are in our own little cells with a past that is seemingly "unrepairable" and unforgivable. We "do our time" outside the grace of Jesus Christ. We find ourselves condemning others for the same sins we've committed ourselves. What prisoners we become when the seeds sown are those sown in bitterness and unforgiveness.

CHAPTER 3

My Favorite Prophet

O ver the past few years, the Lord has placed me in front of criminals who have been abused as children. The statistics are staggering. I've heard that 40% of all criminals were abused as children. I heard another statistic that only 30% of adults that were abused as children come forward. That kind of shoots the first percentage to pieces. If 40% of the criminals only represents the 30% figure over all, we have a serious problem.

Sometimes I feel as if I am a scientist running up and down the halls of a cancer ward with the cure and nobody is listening to me. I compare the sin of sexual abuse to cancer because it literally rots a person to death from the inside out.

A few years ago, I was traveling back to Seattle from Michigan. I decided to take the bus for economic reasons. I was in Chicago awaiting my transfer to another bus and the terminal was packed. I had spent the past three months in Nashville, Michigan and was headed home, I thought, to stay. At that time, I didn't know that I would be returning to Michigan after a semester at United Theological Seminary in Seattle—this time to make it my home.

While sitting in the bus station in Chicago, I was gathering stares from many people. No one came over to talk to me or ask me if I was OK. I began to weep bitterly while thinking in depth about the abuse I went through as a child. I've learned that when God starts doing business with one of His children, He does it when He pleases and where He pleases. Why a bus station? Why in Chicago? Why in front of all these people? I'm not sure about the bus station or Chicago, but I do know "Why in front of all the people". I was being humiliated in front of hundreds of people. All the busy passengers could see were the tears, but my Lord could see the wounds; the lacerations and gashes in my heart that had been covered by lies and more lies. Lies from professionals that were only able to give me Band-aids when what I needed was surgery; surgery from the only one qualified to do the job.

I have always had a thick skull. You know, the "you've got to drill me between the eyes to get my attention" type of skull.

The 53rd chapter of Isaiah came to mind. Why the 53rd chapter of Isaiah? Well, it is my favorite chapter in the whole Bible. Why is it my favorite chapter? I thought it was my favorite chapter because of the 6th verse that reads:

> "We all, like sheep, have gone astray,
> each of us has turned to his own way;
> and the Lord has laid on him
> the iniquity of us all."

Unfortunately, many of the money-making faith healers and other religious groups have distorted and taken out of context the verses in the entire 53rd chapter of Isaiah. Their "name it and claim it" religion has riddled our world with thoughts of scriptural inconsistencies—and in some cases has driven the new believer deeper into his sin-infested dilemma. Sorry to disappoint many of you in the professional field of counseling. The real message in the 53rd chapter of Isaiah isn't one that can be bought, traded, or sold. The message in the 53rd chapter of Isaiah is prophecy. The prophet describes in detail the inward and outward characteristics of Christ, all of which entail the abuse and suffering that Jesus went through—both visible and invisible. Isaiah captures the essence of a Savior suffering and literally dying for a personal relationship with all who invite Him into their heart.

Ever since age eight, when I had been victimized by a warped scout leader, I wanted to tell someone. The anticipated joy of a week-long stay at a boy scout camp had been turned into a nightmare, a silent nightmare, that had more than crippled my self-esteem. The memories followed me and later on in adulthood they remained a crushing blow that paralyzed my relationships with other people. Towards the end of my wretched life of drugs, I was committed by my wife, friends, and relatives to my 4th and final treatment center. I had become obsessed with crack cocaine and a life of just being alone or lying to people so that I could be alone. My trust for people wasn't there and while at this treatment center, my wife (who ended up divorcing me less than a year later) sat across from me with two mediators and informed me that her enjoyment of our physical relationship for the past ten years of marriage had been an act. The head mediator was a professing Christian, highly educated, and attended a very evangelical church. After her comment, the mediator looked at me and informed me that my disease of addiction had infested my intimacy with my wife. I really tried to work his program and placed a ton of confidence in this particular treatment center only to find myself a few months after my discharge to be back on the streets. This time worse than ever. I had a scab that had been picked and my "till death do us part" mate had dealt another blow that left me bleeding to death inside. The thoughts kept playing over and over in my mind like a broken record. The thoughts that over the years had become a faint whisper were now turned up to full volume . . . . YOU'RE DIRTY! YOU'RE DIRTY!

To let you know how far off this therapist was in his comment and partial diagnosis of "my addiction had infested my intimacy", my intimacy was infested long before my addiction came on the scene. I suppose if I had made that fact known to him he would have side stepped the issue like he had everything else about me that didn't fit into his game plan, and probably given the facts another name and then written me off as a statistic. I mean, God forbid that we become really honest and have to face up to the whole truth and nothing but the truth. We may become co-dependent if we start to scripturally care and become aware of the hideous lies that live in the counseling arena today. By the way, I have never been able to find the word co-dependent in scripture. I have read of a man that took on the sins of everyone in the world though. Granted, none of us are saviors, but since when did servanthood take on anything less than pure sacrifice for the sake of others? Why don't we ask the missionary—before he gets burned, battered, or butchered—just how much obedience is worth suffering for? In the counseling arena, and under the definition of co-dependency, that missionary would be the epitome thereof. Let's face it. What modern therapy with a dash of Christianity is building up to is: "A Christ without a cross". Instead of relying on the grace of Christ or the mercy of God, why not rely on some new age counselor who wants to wear the name of Christ but whose counsel doesn't teach the bearing of the pain. Yes, this is where the defense for the new age counselor brings up the most severe cases of abuse to make their case. Among the statistics are lies and exaggerations that are prompted by counselors. The facts are either exaggerated or suppressed. Many victims are more concerned with fitting into a particular mold created by the fallibility of a man just to get an answer—any answer—rather than open themselves up to the truth from their maker. Let's face another fact, the Word of God has never been a real popular alternative when it comes to worldly opinions. If we find our way back to the infallible Word of God, we can read who the father of lies is.

I lived in the counseling scene for 30 years. Many of those years really wanting to be free. I was handed anything and everything in the name of therapy. I've watched its influence increased and the Jesus described in scripture decreased. Over the years I've watched literally hundreds flounder in the depths of the psychological hocus pocus with a dash of Christianity.

The prophet Isaiah described the unglamorous features of Christ in the 53rd chapter. Isaiah also predicted Jesus' death and suffering 740 years before it happened. If you take a real look at that chapter, it also spells out rejection, suffering, and yes—a purpose in all of it. The Son of God, Jesus Christ -the same one who gave me eternal life through the cross—also knew of my abuse and humiliation that had started when I was just a boy undeservedly robbed of my innocence at eight years of age. My Lord held up a mirror image of Calvary in a bus station in Chicago and the Holy Spirit planted deep in my mind the 53rd chapter of Isaiah. There was more than life after death going on there. I love the promise of heaven and eternal life through faith in Jesus Christ but this 53rd chapter of Isaiah tells me in verse 4 that among all this abuse, Dennis Tinsman has someone who is and was willing to take up his infirmities and carry his sorrows. I have someone who was pierced in verse 5 and crushed so that I can have peace. The Son of the Living God, Jesus Christ, knew what it was like to be battered and humiliated in front of a large audience. The people in this Chicago bus station humiliated me. For a few moments, I felt as though they knew about my secret. After that few moments, I quit caring who knew because the only one who really mattered knew all along. My Creator went through abuse that was second to none. Abuse, humiliation, and rejection that was physical, mental, and spiritual so that in verse 10 of the 53rd chapter of Isaiah I can read where the Lord has given a "guilt offering". A guilt offering! No more guilt! It was no longer my abuse but His abuse. I could talk to Jesus and He understood. Jesus, one third of the trinity, relaying to the other two thirds. Now that's what I call a support group!

⁊▲ ⁊▲ ⁊▲ ⁊▲ ⁊▲

Several years ago a piece of paper with writing on it was adopted by a group of men and became a part of the government of our great country. That piece of paper was titled *The Declaration of Independence.*

Since the adoption of that declaration, as a nation we've watched minorities butchered, unborn babies murdered, and homosexuality accepted as an alternate lifestyle. The same governing bodies that accepted *The Declaration of Independence* as valid have now in the name of "A Separation of Church and State" adopted the most immoral and ungodly values.

In the book of Romans, there is another Declaration of Independence written to a church in Rome. This declaration doesn't need the influence of men to make it valid, nor can the truth of its words erode with time. The wisest of men can live by it or perish in spite of it. My choice, and what a choice it is, is to accept it. God's Declaration of Independence is found in Romans, chapter 8, verses 31—39. "What, then, shall we say in response to this? If God is for us, who can be against us? He who did not spare his own Son, but gave him up for us all—how will he not also, along with him, graciously give us all things? Who will bring any charge against those whom God has chosen? It is God who justifies. Who is he that condemns? Christ Jesus, who died—more than that, who was raised to life—is at the right hand of God and is also interceding for us.

Who shall separate us from the love of Christ? Shall trouble or hardship or persecution or famine or nakedness or danger or sword? As it is written:

> 'For your sake we face death
> all day long;
> we are considered as sheep
> to be slaughtered.'

No, in all these things we are more than conquerors through him who loved us. For I am convinced that neither death nor life, neither angels nor demons, neither the present nor the future, nor any powers, neither height, nor depth, nor anything else in all creation, will be able to separate us from the love of God that is in Christ Jesus our Lord."

CHAPTER 4

Pass It On

O kay class, today we are going to play a little game called "Pass It On". It's fun and I think each of us will find a little humor in it. If we all get into a circle and be silent, I'll tell you how to play. Now listen carefully! I am going to whisper a story to Dennis. Dennis will whisper the story to the person next to him, and that person will whisper it to the person next to him or her. We will do this until we have gone around the entire circle. The last person to hear the story will be Peggy. Peggy will then tell the class what she has heard. . . .

"I didn't say that!" was my response to the final link of passed on information that Peggy shared. The rest of the class didn't know that I had a crush on Peggy. I was extremely embarrassed by my outburst. Mrs. Brown smiled and addressed her third grade class with this statement, "Dennis! Everyone has played this game at one time or another. Each of us had fun, and we must play it again sometime." Peggy never spoke to me again. In fact, she avoided me. "Pass It On" was not a pleasant experience for me in the third grade.

I have witnessed, and I'm sure many of you have experienced, the destructive force it has had in families, and in the church. Defeated most by the game is the Christian's testimony for Christ. "Pass It On" cost me a friend in the third grade. I didn't know that someday it would end up costing me my family. Oh, the gossip and meddling are not the issues that destroyed my marriage. They are just small symptoms of a much larger problem within the body of Christ.

The source of the Christian faith and that divine relationship between God and man, through faith in Jesus Christ, is found in the Bible. When a Christian relies on the counsel of anyone, without it being bathed in scripture, he is receiving second-hand information. Maybe they're number five in the circle. Just how distorted is the information? At which point are they in the chain of deception? I was listening to a Christian radio station on my way home from seminary. I almost put my car in the ditch when a well known psychologist, whose ministry I have a great deal of respect for, made a statement—excuse me, several statements—that flashed warning lights on in my heart. I heard a lot of "leave him", "leave her", or the "some make it with this plan, and well, the others they don't". The inconsistencies in this plan are as numerous as those in the life of the carnal Christian. Preaching the good news of eternal life through faith in Jesus Christ used to be the main topic on Christian radio. Now we have general advice or counsel, that could affect families and children for generations, being broadcast in the name of our Lord. Any man can tell us what love must be. In I Corinthians, chapter 13, verses 4—7, God's Word tells us what love *IS*. "Love is patient, love is kind. It does not envy, it does not boast, it is not proud. It is not rude, it is not self seeking, it is not easily angered, it keeps no record of wrongs. Love does not delight in evil but rejoices with the truth. It always protects, always trusts, always hopes, always preserves."

God is uniquely divided into three persons: GOD THE FATHER, GOD THE SON, AND GOD THE HOLY SPIRIT. This is the best team of counselors the Christian has. Isaiah, chapter 28, verse 29 reads like this: "All this also comes from the Lord Almighty, wonderful in counsel and magnificent in wisdom." After all, God designed and made man with a redeemable soul. Even the angels in heaven don't have a redeemable soul. Satan and his demons, which are fallen angels, have their fate sealed. They are unredeemable. Knowing that their fate is sealed, they thrive on redeemable souls receiving ungodly counsel. The sad part in all of this is that a lot of Christians are administering ungodly counsel. I have heard over and over, "Our psychologist says to do it this way." "Their counselor says to do it that way." "So and so did it the other way." We find one person or one family receiving counseling several different ways from numerous individuals. So we have Satan sitting back and saying this: "Okay Christians, today we're going to play a little game called 'Pass It On'. It's smooth and I think you will all find a lot of turmoil in it. If we all get in a circle and be silent, I'll tell you how to play. Now listen carefully. I am going to whisper counsel into this Christian's ear. I'll back it up with scripture. You know, out of context scripture. The same way I did with Jesus. Luke gives an account of my blasphemous use of God's Word in the fourth chapter. Remember when I told your Lord beginning in verse 9: 'If you are the son of God, throw yourself down from here. For it is written: He will command his angels concerning you to guard you carefully; they will lift you up in their hands, so that you will not strike your foot against a stone.' I used this scripture found in Psalm 91, verses 11—12 to try to deceive Jesus. He knew His father's Word because He received it from the source. Jesus refused to play "Pass It On" with me."

I didn't say that! He said . . . ! She said . . . ! The preacher said . . . ! Whatever happened to "thus saith the Lord"? If a person talks to enough people, they can piece together the counsel that best meets their way of thinking, instead of their Lord's will.

Counterfeit counsel is so common and in my estimation is the number one destroyer of the home, the Christians's testimony, and the hope of restoring broken relationships within a family. I look back on numerous counselors (and supposedly godly individuals) whose counsel conveyed everything except the grace that Christ had once offered them. I personally lived in the guilt and condemnation of the game "Pass It On" for the better part of 14 years. Colossians, chapter 4, verse 6 is a refreshing verse that speaks of grace, and of grace that speaks. It reads like this: "Let your conversation be always full of grace, seasoned with salt, so that you may know how to answer everyone."

The U.S. Treasury trains their treasury officers to recognize phony or counterfeit money by studying the real thing. They know what the genuine dollar bill looks and feels like because they've examined it over and over. When handling the distorted, imitation, counterfeit money—no matter how close to genuine it looks or feels—an expert will say, "That's Not It!" The experts learned that studying the various types of deception only confused and frustrated their agents because the variables were so numerous and some counterfeit money was becoming very close to the real thing. With us, instead of looking for the good qualities of counterfeit money, we recognize the bad qualities for what they are. The bottom line is, counterfeit anything just doesn't spend. It's worthless! The person who suffers from counterfeit whatever is the last person to receive it as genuine . . . and later finds out he's been passed a phony.

Paul's letter to the young church of Colosse warned them of counterfeits and philosophical lies. Colossians, chapter 2, verse 8 reads like this: "See to it that no one takes you captive through hollow and deceptive philosophy, which depends on human tradition and the basic principles of this world rather than on Christ."

Dr. James Dobson's ministry has had a tremendous impact in my personal life. His series, *What Wives Wish Their Husbands Knew About Women*, was very significant in the realization of problems that I had brought into my marriage from an extremely abusive childhood. The series also created, through God's grace, a strong willingness to change. My awareness of character traits created from my childhood were made known by the movie and tape series and some principles were applied. However, recognizing those character traits as sin, the divine healing and the assurance of forgiveness were found in a lengthy, daily commitment to God's Word, prayer, and faithfully attending a church; a church that taught of unconditional forgiveness through faith in Jesus Christ. Understanding and memorizing Colossians chapter 1, verses 28 and 29 kept the fire alive in my spirit. It reads like this: "We proclaim him, admonishing and teaching everyone with all wisdom, so that we may present everyone perfect in Christ. To this end I labor, struggling with all his energy, which so powerfully works in me."

Authors and readers of books that counsel in relationships and spiritual matters such as marriage, substance and child abuse, etc., who rely on a book's counsel or passed on information of any type exclusively, will rain sin and destruction on individuals and families. In a marriage situation the two become one. Matthew, chapter 19, verse 6 reads like this: "So they are no longer two but one. Therefore what God has joined together, let man not separate." When counseling with one party in a marriage situation, the counselor is dealing with half of a problem. I would like to see warning labels on books that read, "If divorce, bitterness, or other adverse affects begin to take place, please consult with your Bible for a more personal application from the Holy Spirit."

Much to my dismay, I personally got to witness the results that a single letter brought about. The letter was mailed to a seminary student by some of the leadership in a church he used to attend. The content and accusations crushed this man. The people who mailed the letter reflected back on the man's past and hammered accusations about incidents that he had already confessed to long before. Scripture was used out of context and there was an absolute and blatant disregard for the grace Christ had given this man. Along with the above listed, were hypothetical situations and innuendoes of events that had never taken place. This letter was a prime example and result of the game "Pass It On". One particular quote that stuck in my mind was, "We are tired of your shenanigans."

It was later explained by a friend that shenanigans are a form of "a record of wrongs." Earlier in this chapter, we reflected on scripture found in I Corinthians, chapter 13. At the end of verse 5 we read that "Love keeps no record of wrongs." It was based upon this scripture that his friend explained that if "Love keeps no record of wrongs", then the people who wrote the letter can't scripturally love him. And if they can't scripturally love him, then their problem is really with God. Oh! and what a problem they have. First John, chapter 3, verse 10 reads like this: "This is how we know who the children of God are and who the children of the devil are: Anyone who does not do what is right is not a child of God; nor is anyone who does not love his brother."

Many people in our churches today suffer from what I diagnose as "The Foot And A Half Syndrome". I applied this principle from one of my favorite tracts, *Missing Heaven by 18 Inches*—the distance from the head to the heart. There are a lot of people seeking answers (and missing the help they need spiritually) from counsel that's administered and lacking the identical distance between the same two points.

Circumstances shouldn't dictate obedience to God's Word. Christ, throughout His walk here on earth, looked beyond circumstances and became obedient, even to death. First Peter, chapter 4, verses 16—19 addresses a strong and persevering commitment to the obedience of God's Word. It reads like this: "However, if you suffer as a Christian, do not be ashamed, but praise God that you bear that name. For it is time for judgement to begin with the family of God; and if it begins with us, what will the outcome be for those who do not obey the gospel of God."

All of I and II Peter are good "persevering, in spite of worldly counsel, and choosing to do the right thing" books.

Peter had learned from his early days, when he literally walked next to Christ, that the walk and the submission to God's will go hand in hand. Peter himself was rebuked by Christ. Jesus looked him right in the eyes and rebuked Peter with the words, "Get behind me Satan! You are a stumbling block to me; you do not have in mind the things of God, but the things of man." In the verses preceding Matthew, chapter 16, verse 23, Jesus had explained to Peter God's design and will for His death, burial, and resurrection. Peter didn't have a better plan, he just didn't want to accept God's. How true it is today that the counsel that conflicts with scripture is administered in the name of wisdom; wisdom that isn't from above, yet still administered by people who walk with the Savior.

ᶜᵃ ᶜᵃ ᶜᵃ ᶜᵃ ᶜᵃ

If you wish to emerge as the victor and beat the devil at his own game—the game "Pass It On"—change the rules to: A lengthy, daily commitment to God's Word, prayer, and faithfully attending a church that teaches of unconditional forgiveness through faith in Jesus Christ. Oh, and change the name "Pass It On" to *I Peter, chapter 4, verse 8*. — "Above all love each other deeply, because love covers over a multitude of sins."

CHAPTER 5

My Savior, My Cross

It should have come as no shock to me. It's much easier to read about it and speculate my reaction to it than to recognize it as a necessary part of Christian maturity. There have been times that I have complained about it, lied about it, and I've even gone so far as to blame some of the un-Christlike and humanistic reactions to it on other people. I attend one of those real evangelical churches with a pastor whose views on human problems seem to relate back to the fact that sin is the number one killer of mankind and that Jesus Christ is the only answer for all such problems.

It wouldn't be the first time this Dutchman crucified me in the middle of one of my so-called "down times". I've played golf with him, laughed and joked with him, and consider him one of the most effective tools the Savior has in His service. He started this series on Sunday mornings entitled *The Crucified Life* and literally shredded me on the space in the pew that I occupied.

"Everyone," Pastor stated, "yes, everyone who is a Christian has a cross to carry and there are five things about your cross that I want you to remember:

#1—Everyone has a cross to carry.

#2—Your cross is not the heaviest.

#3—You don't have to carry it alone.

#4—You are to accept it with joy.
#5—Someday you'll get to put it down.

Existing in the temporal standards of the world instead of
God's eternal standards can become mind boggling. One pos-
itively has to have a double standard to exist or try to live in
both worlds. There is not a best of any two worlds collec-
tively, nor is it possible to sit on the fence and live a
crucified life for Christ. No one can be half crucified. A
famous preacher once said, "You can tell when a person is
truly crucified with Christ by these three characteristics:
#1—They're facing in one direction.
#2—They no longer have any plans of their own.
#3—They can never look back."

Author Tim Hensel asked an elderly woman, "Why, if I'm
crucified with Christ, does my old nature keep wiggling?"
The elderly lady responded with: "You must remember, Tim,
crucifixion is a slow death."
A few years ago, the harsh reality of the crucified life came
to me over about a five month time span. The reality
arrived via a middle-aged Baptist preacher, an elderly blind
woman, and the son of evangelist Billy Graham. The middle-
aged Baptist preacher told me in no uncertain terms that I
needed to sew my tongue to the roof of my mouth until I
grew up; the elderly blind woman told me I worried too much
about other people and their opinions; the evangelist's son
told me that servanthood starts with humility.
After surviving the wrath of godly wisdom, I objectively took
a peek at my past and found some very interesting characteristics of my fence sitting, double standard, worldly inflicted values
of life. Manifest in an ungodly foothold from my enemy and
yours, Satan, is the by-product of trying to be holy by the temporal wisdom of the unholy. Check out the four characteristics
of the delusion of an uncrucified life. Perhaps you can evaluate
just how crucified or uncrucified a person is with this scenario:

#1—Woe is me! My cross must be one of the heaviest.

#2—If I lie about my cross, people will think I'm OK.

#3—If I complain about it, God will take it away.

#4 - I can seek blind guidance from people who don't even know what a cross is—thus instilling in my mind the delusion of:

"My cross will never go away."

It's interesting to see how obsessed our society is today with the fix me, fix them, or make us OK with feelings and therapy. The not so harsh reality is that there are some things that will not be OK or fixed until Jesus returns. However, anything apart from God's grace through faith in Jesus Christ is harsh reality. Another absolute is that God tells us through the apostle Paul's experiences that our hurts, hardships, sufferings, addictions, the memories of a bad past (and living with the results of those things) can become our strength in Christ.

Second Corinthians, chapter 12, verses 7—10 reads like this: "To keep me from becoming conceited because of these surpassingly great revelations, there was given me a thorn in my flesh, a messenger of Satan, to torment me. Three times I pleaded with the Lord to take it away from me. But he said to me, 'My grace is sufficient for you, for my power is made perfect in weakness.' Therefore I will boast all the more gladly about my weaknesses, so that Christ's power may rest on me. That is why, for Christ's sake, I delight in weaknesses, in insults, in hardships, in persecutions, in difficulties. For when I am weak, then I am strong."

Jesus' response to Paul goes much deeper than Christ simply saying, "No, I won't take it away." The message is much deeper than Christ's strength being manifested in weakness. It's that thorn in the flesh (the hurts, the hardships, and the sufferings) that made Paul the magnificent man of God that he was. The essence of who Paul was in Christ became reality through him as a child of God suffering through trials and an unchangeable thorn in the flesh. The brokenness of a man;

a brokenness that only Christ Himself could understand. Would Paul have longed so deeply to be with his Lord and Savior Jesus Christ if his life after conversion had been one big glory trail without suffering? Could he have focused so richly on his ministry? Paul's words to the Philippians in chapter 1, verse 21 says, "For to me, to live is Christ, and to die is gain." Yes, God's grace through Paul's faith in Jesus Christ was sufficient. That depth of love, compassion, and understanding is still alive today. I believe the surrounding verses to "My grace is sufficient", and inclusive of, is a message from Christ to Paul that says this: "I know, Paul, about the crucified life. I wrote the book on it. If I take away your cross, it would ruin you. You must understand, Paul, I created you for my glory, not yours. I love you and it's that thorn in your flesh that keeps you dependent upon me. It's that thorn in your flesh, those trials and past memories, along with my mercy and grace, that have made you the finest apostle that has ever come after me. Your words in me and my Word in you, will be written and read into eternity. Your writings will become a part of my book, *The Holy Bible*. Millions will be saved and spend eternity with their Savior because of your dependency on me. You see, Paul, your cross isn't the heaviest; Mine was."

ॐ ॐ ॐ ॐ ॐ

It has been said, "There's no honor among thieves." I ask you: Is there honor among thieves? . . . Yes, I believe there is. For amidst the company of thieves, there hung on a cross a Savior. This picture of Calvary is painted into all eternity. The words of one particular criminal read, "We hang here for our crimes; for what our deeds deserve. But this man Jesus has done nothing wrong." There was no time left for confirmation, good works, or even a baptism. Yet in a moment's decision, the eternity of one man was decided; a man known simply as a criminal. The Savior looked at this rejected member of society and his repentant spirit and so stated, "Today you will be with me in Paradise." Yes, somewhere in the presence of the Lord is a thief, a murderer, a liar, a conniver, a manipulator, and a back -stabber who's kicking up his heels as he rejoices in the blood of his newly-found friend, Jesus Christ. A friend named Jesus that this criminal literally "hung around" just a few moments before death. I ask you again . . . Is there honor among thieves?

It's Not My Fault

I was leading a seminar in a county jail in Northern Michigan. The jail rented space out to neighboring courts and law enforcement agencies. The seminar was a Life Plan Seminar and was designed to assist inmates as they were released back into society. The seminar had clear and concise overtones of assuming responsibility for one's own actions. My years as a criminal, a drug addict, a drunk, and a bitter human being have lead me into the realm of being very direct. I am a firm believer that "it's the Truth that sets men free". I believe our society today, with its modern, new age counseling, alleviates the responsibility one feels for their actions. One pastor describes sin as an erosion process. After many years, our system has learned to talk in psychological circles to justify or explain away people's sinful actions. The gorges and "Grand Canyons" in people's lives become the tragedies that find their way into other people's lives. Those "other people" are known as victims. If the victims survive, they somehow make their own victims and those victims make their own victims and well, it's really nobody's fault . . . . or is it?

I recall a judge's comments that were made public by way of the local newspaper. After the sentencing of a sex offender, who had made his victim a fourteen year old boy, the judge had this to say in light of all the letters written by church members on behalf of the accused: "Those of you who believe in the innocence of the accused are sadly mistaken. Those of you who think that the fact that the accused was himself a victim of a similar crime and that fact should dismiss him of his responsibility in this case, are wrong." The judge went on to say, "I can't imagine anyone who had been through a similar experience would want to inflict that type of behavior on anyone else."

Along with pornography, immorality, and the sexual abuse that's running rampant across our country, we seem to pass on the excuses and self-justification of the most hideous crimes.

I am not sure where the bravery comes from. Is it the by-product of my many close calls with death? Perhaps the boldness I feel when expressing my Lord to the lost is an unshakable faith from God that is amplified by the empathy I have with convicted felons who are facing life sentences. This particular situation was unexpected and for a county jail scene it was not what I was prepared for. I use every jail situation, every prison situation, and the victims involved as illustrations for numerous environments that the ministry leads me to. However, the Life Plan Seminar seemed awfully bleak for one inmate. I was filling out the certificates for the in-prison seminar while the jail chaplain was teaching a budget plan for inmates. While he was putting the finishing touches on the ten hour seminar, I was repetitiously signing the certificates of completion. Most of the jail inmates were sentenced to one year or less in the county jail and there was a mixture of men and women. They were mostly gang members and prostitutes off the streets of Detroit. Just about all of them had severe drug habits. I've learned to be flexible in prison ministry and adapt to the various audiences. The message stays the same but the delivery may vary as the Spirit leads.

Directly across from the room I had been lecturing in was a large man. I should say a huge man. I'm about six foot tall and weigh 220 lbs. but this guy's size seemed to dwarf me. I

"We hang here for our crimes; for what our deeds deserve.
But this man Jesus has done nothing wrong."

had to walk right past his observation cell during the two days that I was scheduled to be at this facility. He was under 24 hour observation and I could tell that this guy was not part of the normal jail activities. I kept glancing into the isolation cell as I typed each name on the certificates. I was about finished and I asked the jailor on duty, "What's the story on that guy?" "That guy? That guy!" he responded, "is a mean one." Looking for more specifics, I inquired, "And what makes that guy such a mean one? How come he's not at the Life Plan Seminar?" The deputy looked at me and stated, "The only life plan that man will ever see is the one he's in right now. How many people have you ever met, Dennis, that were able to blow their own parents away and then turn themselves in?" A lump came to my throat and tears began to erupt from my eyes.

"Can he have visitors?" I asked. "Yes," the jailor responded, "he gets one visit per week for one hour. Some Jehovah's Witness guy shows up. We shackle Bill's hands and legs together and he and his preacher friend meet in private in the room over there. Bill has been here one year now with all the trial procedures and competency hearings. I don't believe that old Jehovah's Witness character has ever missed a lick." "What would it take to get me in to talk with him?" I asked. The jailor explained to me that he would have to lock me inside the isolation cell. Yep! You guessed it! Just me and Bill and nowhere to hide. I agreed that before I went in to visit him I would read some of the news clippings. I sat at the jailor's desk and read numerous newspaper articles on Bill and my periodical glances at him kept me asking the question: Why? I prayed and asked the Lord to help me park my curiosity outside. The jailor gave me 30 minutes with Bill and I wanted to share Christ with him and not satisfy my more than inquisitive attitude. My prayer for our meeting went something like this:

"Dear Jesus, I don't understand Bill's crime, but you do. I've read in your Word, Jesus, about all the bad people you talked with in person. Jesus, I'm not a very discerning person, so you'll have to give me discernment. I'm not a patient man and the last time I asked you for patience, Lord, I found myself up to my neck in trials. Jesus, if you will help me see Bill the way you do, I believe my words will be yours. Please, Holy Spirit, move in Bill's heart. I know for the past year Bill has been hearing religion. A religion that doesn't teach that you are The Way, The Truth, and The Life. Please, Lord, let me be your ambassador and not the advocate of any religion. In Jesus name, Amen."

I never asked the Lord to protect me. I believe the physical man to be second to the spiritual man. I believe that message was made clear at the cross. I consider myself a missionary and hang onto the scripture that says our fight isn't with flesh and blood, but the principalities of darkness. I thank the Lord for His protection, but I just can't bring myself to ask Him for it for myself. Those of you who know my past know that there were many times the Lord delivered me even when I didn't care about me. I feel like it would be an unintentional slam to my very faithful Lord.

I watched as the jailor went down to Bill's private cell. They exchanged words through a feeding port in the steel door. The slot was big enough to pass a tray through. I watched as Bill went into his sleeping area and the door shut behind him. The jailor motioned for me to come down and as I entered the small area, I looked back through the thick glass window where I had been sitting—typing and signing certificates. I tried to picture myself the way Bill saw me just moments ago. I had a copy of my book, *A Garment of Grace*, in my hand and I sat down at the table in Bill's miniature combination living room and dining room. The furniture was a table and attached stools. They were bolted to the floor and wall and were more a part of the structure than they were pieces of furniture. For Bill, this had been home for the past year. The remote door opened and Bill joined me and sat directly across from me. He wasted no time striking up a conversation.

Bill: What do you want? What's the book?

Me: I'm an ex-convict and I wrote this book. I am affiliated with prison ministry and I'm leading a seminar across the hall. I thought perhaps you would like a copy of my book and to talk with someone.

Bill: How much for the book?

Me: It's free!

Bill: Nothing's free! How much?

Me: I suppose your right. I tell you what, you read it and send me a letter telling me what you think of me as a writer. You can critique my writing. Bill took the book and I autographed it for him. After a moment of silence, the conversation began again.

Bill: So, you're an ex-con huh?! How much time do I have to do?

Me: I'm a firm believer in being honest, Bill. Your crime is serious. And if I were you, I'd be more concerned with your actions and not your sentence. The state will probably have you for a long, long time.

Bill: It's not my fault you know. I am a schizophrenic.

Me: I'm not real up on big words. You'll probably get that after you read my book. What makes you a schizophrenic?

Bill spent the next five minutes giving me a clinical description of himself; he had all the bits and pieces of his psychological profile in order. His understanding of himself as described by his defense, well, he had the script down pat. One thing for sure; Bill was convinced that he could pick up a rifle, load it, chamber a round, and shoot his mom. Then he could chamber another round, take aim, and shoot his dad—and according to his psychological profile, it's not his fault. There were few questions in my mind. I guess the only question that lingered, that I didn't ask, seemed to be irrelevant at this time. I was curious why a psychiatrist would order medication for Bill's mental state. The same medication Bill had been on for years to deal with his mood swings. Yet in order for Bill to stand trial for murdering his parents, at his competency hearing the judge ordered him off the mind- and mood-altering drugs. Wading through the confusion of Bill's situation, I had one question that needed to be asked and time was running out. That question: Where will Bill spend eternity? I jumped right into the heart of Bill's problems without knowing it. Thank you, Holy Spirit!

Me: Did you go to church as a boy, Bill?

Bill: Yes, we went to several churches.

Me: When you say "we", who are you talking about?

Bill: My mom, my dad and me. We tried the Methodists, then we tried the Lutherans and then the Baptists. My parents couldn't get along with the people at any of the churches. We stayed at one church for almost two years, but my parents got mad at some of the people. That was the last church we went to.

Me: How old were you, Bill, when you stopped going to church?

Bill: Fourteen.

Me: Then what happened?

Bill: About six months later I started smoking pot and then a few months later I was taking L.S.D.

Me: How long did your drug abuse last?

Bill: Many, many years. I finally started getting prescription drugs for my mood swings.

Me: Have you ever heard of Jesus Christ, Bill, and what it means to be saved?

Bill: I believe Jesus Christ was probably the greatest man that ever lived but that's all He was—just a man.

Me: If Jesus Christ was only a great man, Bill, where does that leave you as a murderer?

Bill: I don't know.

Me: Who told you that you weren't responsible for your actions?

Bill: My therapist.
Me: Suppose he's wrong?
Bill: He's not.
Me: Just suppose he is.
Bill: I said he's not!
Me: Bill, when do you start taking responsibility for your actions?
Bill: I think it's time for you to leave.
Me: I think you're right.

I couldn't help the despair I was feeling. As I exited his cell, he pleasantly said good-bye and assured me that he would read my book and write me. I have yet to hear from him. I suppose for Bill—in his mind—if he has no sin, he has no need for a savior. As long as Bill has a religion without a relationship to Christ, he will be able to fulfill all his mental requirements but his soul will be eternally damned. I have prayed for Bill's salvation when the Lord brings him to mind. I have asked God to somehow let me know if he gets saved.

"It's Not My Fault." I hear those words a lot lately. Our entire country has given way to that ungodly plague. Our churches and Christian communities have done the same. I believe the newspapers that reported Bill's tragedy got one date wrong. Perhaps the slowest bullets I've ever heard of made their way to Bill's mom and dad. You see, I believe that the shots were fired the day Bill's parents walked away from God. The erosion process for Bill's family took twenty years and became a gorge, a Grand Canyon. Yes, a huge void that was filled with animosity, bitterness, and hate that found its victims in the form of two bullets. And, well, it's really nobody's fault. Or is it?

CHAPTER 7

1 John 1:9, God's
Three Step Program

Drug and alcohol centers, hospitals, retirement homes,
and prisons are looked upon as the ultimate in
depression, pain, and grief. I guess you can say, "It's
all in the heart of the beholder." Since Jesus is holding this
heart, the institutions I listed are an opportunity for encouragement, healing, and most of all—sharing the Savior with
those in need. I had done my time in all of the above except
retirement homes. As an inmate or patient, I saw them as
places I never wanted to return to. I look at them now as the
melting pot for salvation or an environment of perseverance
for one's recommitment to Jesus Christ.

I was upset, to say the least, at the professionals' worldly
views on the patients and their problems. I was even more
upset when I heard the patients' outlooks on their counselors, psychiatrists, and duty nurses. I had been visiting a
friend at a combination psychiatric unit and drug-alcohol
rehabilitation center. This unit is known as one of the best
in the state. The people on staff there told me how both the
facility and its employees were held in high esteem throughout the state. As I listened to the patients describe their
problems ranging from suicide to substance abuse, I
thought to myself, "Best in which state and best compared

71

to what?" The patients were bragging about how they were manipulating the staff.

One lady there called me at home because she couldn't talk to her assigned counselor. She told me that the staff said they were going to send her to a maximum security facility if she didn't start talking in group therapy. Betty called to inform me that she was going to finish the job when she got out. Betty announced, "I'll play their little games and when they release me, I'll finish the job. It's my right! It's my life, and I'm sick of it. I don't feel! I don't want to feel! I am beyond feeling! I don't care!" As you can probably tell by reading, Betty was committed for a suicide attempt. She was 30 years old and had three children, ages four, six, and seven. My heart started aching for her and I prayed, "Lord, let Betty open up to me." As our phone conversation went on, she shared with me how her older brother had raped her when she was nine years old. She told me this: "I don't have time for religion. My brother is now a prominent member and deacon in his church."

I shared with Betty that we have a mutual friend named Jesus who isn't fond of hypocritical religious leaders. I responded with, "Your brother may or may not have asked for forgiveness. Regardless, you must forgive him, love him, and let Jesus Christ take care of the rest." I consoled her with the fact that she didn't have to run a game on Jesus to get the peace she was looking for. I told her she could feel again. "You must be searching for something," I reported, "or you wouldn't have bothered calling me!" After a moment of silence, Betty shared with me that she accepted Christ ten years ago. I about dropped the phone. Betty then proceeded to tell me that she and her husband had been attending a local Christian Church. I was speechless. Betty then blurted out, "You don't understand!" I answered with this, "Oh! But I do. I understand all too well. I was sexually abused as a child, emotionally abused by relatives, and I can only tell you about what has made the change in me—and it wasn't killing myself. Betty, if you take your life you know you're going to face your Lord. You don't want to meet

Him face to face that way. God can use you just the way you are. Jesus does His best work in and through Christians who give up on themselves. When we give up on ourselves, then we can start putting our confidence and trust in Jesus."

Betty knew that I liked to write and express my Lord and my innermost self on paper. I encouraged her to write everything down. I instructed her, "Write about anything that comes to mind. I'll come up and visit you tomorrow and you can share with me what you've got. I like it when people express themselves on paper."

The next day I was visiting another patient there and Betty came up to me. She was smiling. She handed me a piece of paper and said, "Here it is. I hope you can understand it. It is all I could think of!" I took the single notebook-style piece of paper from Betty and excused myself by telling her, "I want to go off alone and read this."

As I started reading Betty's story, an overwhelming feeling of peace came over me. I started crying. Betty was expressing the exact same feelings I once had. For a person who said she couldn't feel—and didn't want to feel—she seemed to be doing an awfully good job of expressing deep, deep feelings on this piece of paper that I was holding. Betty has given me permission to share her expressions of hurt and rejection. This is the exact copy of what Betty wrote:

Picture this you and me
walking down a white sand beach
We're holding hands, the warm wind blows
We're all alone, All the dreams are
fantasies they're not real. Not reality!
And now I cry over you, Nearly die over
you. All the bits and pieces of us that
I try to find are only faded memories
of another place and time. We were
as happy as can be. You *were* loving me.
Now it's just an image that I find

when you left I fell apart. I was torn
You broke my heart, Now I cry over you
Nearly die over you.
Impressions of the way it was long ago,
Somewhere back in time . . .

In addition to being sexually abused as a child, Betty had
been sexually assaulted two years earlier at gunpoint.

Betty's husband had filed for divorce a few days before her
suicide attempt and admittance to this facility. Betty was feeling! Betty was feeling the epitome of rejection, humiliation,
and absolute worthlessness. Betty wasn't focusing in on anything but her latest tragedy, *Divorce!*

Betty had been able to accept and stand up under the system of the courts. She shared with me how the legal system
made her out to be the criminal and how her perpetrator was
the victim. Here stood Betty two years later dealing with the
same system that stripped her of her dignity, her family, and
her desire to live.

I couldn't share too much with Betty about our Lord Jesus;
the Jesus she had once asked into her heart. They were very
strict in this so-called "top notch" psychiatric ward.

I had manipulated counselors for years. The only wisdom
I couldn't manipulate was the wisdom found in God's Word.
I couldn't get burned out on it either. Instead of suppressing
symptoms like the world does, I found absolute healing inside
from an extremely abusive childhood. I was able to express
secrets that had devastated me. Mixing worldly counsel with
Christ doesn't work. Counselors of the world glory in
themselves, their programs, and their successes. I have seen
them suppress their failures. I have witnessed people being
treated like guinea pigs. You know, the old, "try this on this
group and in a few months or years we can check the statistics". I wonder what Christ is feeling when all this blasphemy
is going on? He isn't going to go to the cross again! God's
Word is specific on sin and the results of sin. Forgiveness and

grace must go hand in hand. One must wonder about I John, chapter 1, verse 9 when we read that we are cleansed from some unrighteousness; excuse me, God says from *all* unrighteousness. Who do we believe? When spiritual ailments result in sin, there isn't anything short of Jesus Christ to remedy those results. When physical ailments take place or are present, God's grace through faith in Jesus Christ is the only hope. For years, friends and family (who are professing Christians) had referred me to programs and counselors that were deep in their knowledge, well educated with their degrees, and had all the answers to keep me dwelling on the past and rehashing over and over the guilt that almost killed me.

I was a crack cocaine addict. The amount of cocaine I did was enough to do permanent brain damage. I was told by experts that the neuro-transmitters in my brain were damaged and my pleasure center would be a long time returning to anything close to normal. I was told that I was stuck with this as well as a lifetime commitment to meetings that told me I had given myself a disease called addiction. I had been to several treatment centers and I lived in constant fear of that little white rock. I dwelled on it, worried about it, and after 1 1/2 years, I returned to it . . . giving up my faith in Christ, my family, and the hope of happiness through the worldly counsel I mixed with Jesus Christ. God showed me through an 83 year old lady and a 52 year old preacher just what Jesus Christ was all about. I had the Living Answer inside me for 16 years and I tried to separate Jesus from my alcohol and drug addiction. Three months after my total commitment to Christ and a total rejection of any type or form of worldly counsel, I found myself in seminary headed for full-time ministry. My grade point average was 3.7. Seven months after my commitment I had written and completed my first book, *A Garment Of Grace*, and was three chapters deep in the book you're reading now. I have walked with addicts and ministered to them. I don't fear that little white rock. Cocaine is *The*

Small Lie. *The Big Lie* is that the addiction is incurable. One of my favorite scripture verses is Colossians, chapter 2, verses 13—15. It reads like this: "When you were dead in your sins and in the uncircumcision of your sinful nature, God made you alive with Christ. He forgave us all our sins, having canceled the written code, with its regulations, that was against us and that stood opposed to us; he took it away, nailing it to the cross. And having disarmed the powers and authorities, he made a public spectacle of them, triumphing over them by the cross." This is Paul's expression of Christ's victory over death in the light of worldly wisdom. I am no longer powerless over the little white rock. Crack cocaine has no power when it comes to my *Eternal Rock: Jesus Christ*.

I love my new life. I asked that 52 year old preacher what I needed to change. He said, "Everything!" That was almost four years ago. My Lord has changed everything and has been restoring the important things in my life. Two of those important things are my two children. I haven't seen my son or daughter in almost four years. The beauty in all of it is: THEY'RE SAVED! I'll get to spend eternity with them.

When a person finds his or her answers to healing exclusively in Jesus Christ, the Lord gets the glory and the godly source is looked upon as a messenger or tool for their Lord. First John, chapter 1, verse 9 is a three step program. It reads like this: Step one, "If we confess our sins," Step two, "he is faithful and just and will forgive us our sins," Step three, "and purify us from all unrighteousness."

I recall a poster a former employer of mine had on his office wall. It pictured a huge ocean liner being dwarfed by waves in the midst of a storm at sea. Inscribed at the bottom of the picture were these words:

> The Lord doesn't always calm
> the storm:
> He sometimes calms His child while
> the storm rages on.

❒ ❒ ❒ ❒ ❒

How can a person direct someone to the answer if they are ignorant to the cure; or if they don't have the Living Answer in themselves?

CHAPTER 8

The Fountain: A Spring of Living Water

Excuse me, could you tell me when the fountain will be operating again? I had interrupted a construction worker with these words. It was a sunny day in May and I was anxious to experience the peaceful, elegant, and enriching feelings that this water wonder known as a fountain was capable of producing. I envisioned the fountain's flourishing waters shooting skyward with the same driven force of grandeur as the summer before.

I questioned the construction worker as to the task he was performing and asked him why a fountain that had only been around a short while was under such extensive repair.

"By the way, what is your name?" he asked. "Dennis," I replied. "Well Dennis," he began to explain, "as you can see, the mason who installed the tile work and the inlaid designs did a magnificent job. The landscaper who planted and arranged the garden surrounding us had a real mind for beauty. The person who donated the fountain went first class and invested a fortune in it. The concrete walkways are as smooth as silk. The finisher had a unique touch with a trowel. I can't imagine," he continued, "why someone would allow a plumber to come in and use such inferior materials and do such a poor job installing what he thought no one else would ever see."

I knew nothing about plumbing a fountain, or anything else he was talking about, before this encounter. However, by the time he was finished explaining, I could tell you what should have been done and what was needed to repair and make anew this gushing aquatic pool of beauty.

This construction expert went on to tell me, "It was bad enough using this cheap material, but along with the improper installation, well Dennis, . . . it's a shame; a darn shame. Look here," he pointed out, "the piping is worthless for this type of application. The proper plumbing material should be a high grade, pressure resistant type that is planted deep enough so that the weather won't destroy it. One good freeze and it's all over for this stuff." "What do you do now?" I asked. "You leave the old plumbing right where it is," he answered, "and run new plumbing to the fountain deep enough so that the weather won't get to it." "Why don't you dig up the old material and replace it with the new?" I questioned. "What for?" he asked. "I can install a new pipeline without digging up and ruining the existing garden, tile, or concrete work. Once the new pipeline is hooked up, the old plumbing is there but it becomes a part of the ground. The only ones who know it's there are you, me, the good Lord, and if this fountain had a mind, it would know. It's not going to affect the way the water shoots out of the nozzles if the old stuff is no longer a part of the plumbing."

I find it interesting, to say the least, what scripture says in Matthew, chapter 10, verse 28: "Do not be afraid of those who kill the body but cannot kill the soul. Rather, be afraid of the one who can destroy both soul and body in hell." These are the words of the Savior Himself. Notice how Jesus gives only two options. He is interested in one thing: the soul of man. In the preceding verse, Jesus is addressing His second coming and explaining what things will be like. Families will be against their own families, as we read in Matthew, chapter 10, verse 21. Jesus goes a little further and addresses us in verses 24—26 of the same chapter in Matthew with, "A student is not above his master. It is enough for the student to be like his teacher, and the servant like his master. If the head of the house has been called Beelzebub, how much more the members of his household. So don't be afraid of them. There is nothing concealed that will not be disclosed, or hidden that will not be made known."

If a student is not above his teacher, then the counseled is not above his counselor. The counseled, if receiving ungodly counsel, is literally at the mercy of his counselor and is unaware of the deceiving satanic influence that's being imbedded in his heart and mind which were meant for holiness. Ungodly counsel is any counsel that distorts, compromises, or conflicts with scripture in any way, shape, or form. The recipient of ungodly counsel becomes like the fountain; a beautiful work of their Heavenly Father and dedicated by the blood of Jesus. Satan becomes a plumber and installs trash that is, but never was meant to be, part of God's beautiful creation. The counseled looks beautiful for a season. The real by-product of this hideous workmanship goes unnoticed because it's buried where no one can see it. The blessings that once gushed from his heart, reached to the heavens, and were enjoyed by everyone have ceased and the person becomes an obstacle that takes up space. Proverbs, chapter 18, verse 4 reads like this: "The words of a man's mouth are deep waters, but the fountain of wisdom is a bubbling brook."

Every person has pain, trials, and suffering in their life at one time or another. When their plumbing is exposed to any of these things, the true quality of the material and the depth of the installation is revealed. When the Holy Spirit becomes the plumber and God's Word becomes the material—along with the depth of installation being an absolute faith in Jesus Christ -this Christian will maintain unconditional obedience to his Lord. He will project, through his attitude, an inner peace free of accusations against others and will see his circumstances as being an opportunity for Jesus Christ to reveal

Himself. After all, Jesus Christ and the Holy Spirit, along with their Father in Heaven, did a beautiful job on the rest of the creation. God knows what type of material a fountain needs and how important the depth is in order to withstand the weathery trials we experience. Psalms, chapter 36, verse 9 reads like this: "For with you is the fountain of life; in your light we see light."

If you've tried the rest, now try the best: read God's Word daily, pray regularly, and faithfully attend a church that teaches of unconditional forgiveness through faith in Jesus Christ.

I, myself, being a fountain that had every type of plumbing tried on me, finally, by the grace of God, got all the right material and used just one plumber . . . *The Holy Spirit*. He never did remove all that old worthless inferior stuff. I suppose He left it there so that I could tell you just how poorly it worked. The only people who know about it are God, myself, and everyone who was around me for 29 years watching the praises and blessings stop. I have been told by God's Word (now that all the right stuff is inside me) the only things that matter are the praises going upward from all directions—and the blessings are showers at the end of those praises. The blood of the Savior covers all of that old shallow worthless material.

ॐ ॐ ॐ ॐ ॐ

Zechariah, chapter 13, verses 1 and 2: "'On that day a fountain will be opened to the house of David and the inhabitants of Jerusalem, to cleanse them from sin and impurity. On that day, I will banish the names of the idols from the land, and they will be remembered no more,' declares the Lord Almighty, 'I will remove both the prophets and the spirit of impurity from the land.'"

CHAPTER 9

The Toughman Gym

For three bucks a week you can visit The Toughman Gym. It's open twenty-four hours a day, Monday through Thursday. The hours on Fridays and Saturdays are from 6 a.m. to 6 p.m. The Toughman Gym is closed on Sundays. Doug told me the reason that he charges only three bucks a week is to maintain the facility. You can go as often as you wish and stay as long as you like. There are no earrings allowed and if you deliberately damage or vandalize the property in The Toughman Gym, your medical insurance best be paid up. I have seen the owner work out. Even in his late fifties, Doug still hits the heavy punching bag with an enthusiasm that makes it dance like a rag doll. His pulverizing of this punching bag reminds me of a line in an old song sung by Tennessee Ernie Ford titled Sixteen Tons. A line in the song states: "If the right one don't get you, then the left one will."

Among the weights, exercise machines, and punching bags, are warning signs, along with cleverly worded posters, hung strategically around the gym. They express a criteria of dos and don'ts. Within the message of the dos and don'ts are clearly expressed results of what will happen if you fail to heed the instructions of safety or are found breaking the rules. The expressed results are explained as: (A) self inflicted, caused by the victim's stupidity or (B) the blatant disregard for the rules

85

may warrant great physical pain inflicted by the owner. Any type of infringement of the property or misuse of the gym is discouraged. Graphically described in the wording of these warning signs and posters are the implied results for those who take for granted in any way, shape, or form—The Toughman Gym.

One of the signs on the wall of The Toughman Gym reads like this: "Remember the Golden Rule! Whoever has the Gold makes the Rules." I had never heard this pronunciation, interpretation, or application of The Golden Rule. I remember one form of The Golden Rule being worded like this: "Do unto others as you would have others do unto you." Still another form is worded and has a sort of rhythmic or poetic ring to it. The wording goes something like this: "Be unto others kind and true as you would have others be unto you." However, the statement "Whoever has the Gold makes the Rules" clearly establishes the ownership and the authority of that ownership of The Toughman Gym.

Not all of the signs and posters, along with their cleverly worded cliches, refer to safety rules or the breaking of those rules. One such sign is small and has been placed directly above the heavy punching bag. Its message is direct, profound, and is administered to the reader as a point of view from one's past experiences. The small sign reads like this: "It's better to have less thunder in the mouth and more lightning in the hand."

The poster with the strongest meaning, and the finalization of its implied results, seems a bit drastic. It reads like this: "If you're found here tonight, you'll be found here in the morning." The message in this is strong. However, the illustration next to it captures one's attention and drives the point directly into the mind. They say "a picture paints a thousand words". The picture on this poster paints few words. When you look at the words, "If you're found here tonight, you'll be found here in the morning", you are also staring down the barrel of a very large pistol. In fact, the frontal view of this pistol, at the scale it was illustrated, makes it look like a cannon with six shots. The artist was very graphic in his illustration of this pistol and made it so that it took up more space on the poster than the large print words did. The words this picture paints simply state, "YOU'RE DEAD!"

It is evident that every poster, with its strategic location, had a purpose—and they entertained me with humor the first time I read them. After spending a lot of time in this gym at late night hours, lifting weights and listening to a Christian radio station, I began matching up the signs and posters, along with their cleverly worded cliches, with the songs, sermons, and scripture that were being broadcast. I started applying the warnings and profound statements to situations in and around my life. I realized that the Bible has several such warnings and many of the biblical warnings are just as profound. The Word of God certainly is sharper than any two-edged sword.

For some people, there are certain unfortunate examples of unheeded warnings that result in tragedy. For others, who seem to be on an awfully long leash, one might wonder just what the response will be when the owner returns.

Although unsaved as a boy, I learned a song in Sunday school titled *This Is My Father's World*. One of the lines in the song reads: "This is my Father's world and to my listening ears all nature sings and around me rings the music of the sphere." Few people today have "listening ears" that are sensitive to the godliness that is in the Bible. Their listening ears have switched frequency and now absorb the lies and perversions of a gradually declining lifestyle of the ungodly.

In Romans, chapter 1, verses 20—32, the scriptures tell us God's outlook on a defiled, demanding, and disobedient people. Romans, chapter 1, verses 20—32, reads like this: "For since the creation of the world, God's invisible qualities—his eternal power and divine nature—have been clearly seen, being understood from what has been made, so that men are without excuse.

For although they knew God, they neither glorified him as God nor gave thanks to him, but their thinking became futile and their foolish hearts were darkened. Although they claimed to be wise, they became fools and exchanged the glory of the immortal God for images made to look like mortal man and birds and animals and reptiles.

Therefore God gave them over in the sinful desires of their hearts to sexual impurity for the degrading of their bodies with one another. They exchanged the truth of God for a lie, and worshiped and served created things rather than the Creator—who is forever praised. Amen.

Because of this, God gave them over to shameful lusts. Even their women exchanged natural relations for unnatural ones. In the same way the men also abandoned natural relations with women and were inflamed with lust for one another. Men committed indecent acts with other men, and received in themselves the due penalty for their perversion.

Furthermore, since they did not think it worthwhile to retain the knowledge of God, he gave them over to a depraved mind, to do what ought not to be done. They have become filled with every kind of wickedness, evil, greed and depravity. They are full of envy, murder, strife, deceit and malice. They are gossips, slanderers, God-haters, insolent, arrogant and boastful; they invent ways of doing evil; they disobey their parents; they are senseless, faithless, heartless, ruthless. Although they know God's righteous decree that those who do such things deserve death, they not only continue to do these very things but also approve of those who practice them."

The Bible is full of the accounts of religious people who, in the past, have failed to heed the warnings of an all-loving and all-forgiving God through faith in Jesus Christ. The apostle Paul correlates these warnings from man's past history with the present day man and the entire future of mankind.

Jesus tells us He is going to return like a thief in the night. Luke, chapter 12, verses 39 and 40, reads like this: "But understand this: If the owner of the house had known at what hour the thief was coming, he would not have let his house be broken into. You also must be ready, because the Son of Man will come at an hour when you do not expect him." First Thessalonians, chapter 5, verses 1—3, reads like this: "Now, brothers, about times and dates we do not need to write to you, for you know very well that the day of the Lord will come like a thief in the night. While people are saying, 'Peace and safety,' destruction will come on them suddenly, as labor pains on a pregnant woman, and they will not escape." Revelation, chapter 16, verse 15, reads like this: "Behold, I come like a thief! Blessed is he who stays awake and keeps his clothes with him, so that he may not be naked and be shamefully exposed."

It would be great to see signs (like the one in The Toughman Gym which states, "If you're found here tonight, you'll be found here in the morning") at the entrances to pornography stores, night clubs, prostitution houses, drug houses, counselors and counseling centers; those places which undermine the power of Christ. Many professing Christians frequent such establishments. In order for a Christian to get the new mind we read about in Romans, chapter 12, verse 2, one must repent and turn from such sin. "Do not conform any longer to the pattern of this world, but be transformed by the renewing of your mind. Then you will be able to test and approve what God's will is—his good, pleasing and perfect will." There is not an addiction to anything that is not completely curable by God through faith in Jesus Christ. The modern psychotherapy either dilutes the authority of Jesus Christ or eliminates Him completely from its counsel. More than being riddled with biblical inconsistencies, most of the worldly counsel today has become so bold as to reject the Savior by implying that Christ is merely a rightful opinion of someone. Many Christian counselors, therapists, psychologists, psychiatrists, and their places of practice have adopted the world's methods and have inserted Jesus as a necessary part of their program. What ever happened to the Holy Spirit? Since when did worldly opinions have the keys to unlock a person's hardened and calloused heart caused by sin?

"It's better to have less thunder in the mouth and more lightning in the hand". The words of that sign (from the wall of The Toughman Gym) directly relate to trying to find healing in the vacant words used by the unsaved counselor, or even a saved counselor, as well as the teachings of an unsaved teacher or professor. The Christian community, our churches especially, must grab onto God's Word and hold fast. God denounced, through the prophet Isaiah, the policies of the wise. Isaiah, chapter 29, verses 13—16, reads like this:

> "The Lord says:
> 'These people come near to me
> with their mouth
> and honor me with their lips,
> but their hearts are far from me.
> Their worship of me
> is made up only of rules taught
> by men.
> Therefore once more I will astound
> these people
> with wonder upon wonder;
> the wisdom of the wise will perish,
> the intelligence of the intelligent
> will vanish.'
> Woe to those who go to great depths
> to hide their plans from the
> Lord,
> who do their work in darkness and
> think,
> 'Who sees us? Who will know?'
> You turn things upside down,
> as if the potter were thought to be
> like the clay!
> Shall what is formed say to him

who formed it,
'He did not make me'?
Can the pot say of the potter,
'He knows nothing'?'"
The apostle Paul forwarded the words of the Lord through the prophet Isaiah and expanded on them in I Corinthians, chapter 1, verses 18—25. It reads like this: "For the message of the cross is foolishness to those who are perishing, but to us who are being saved it is the power of God. For it is written:

'I will destroy the wisdom of
the wise;
the intelligence of the
intelligent I will
frustrate.'

Where is the wise man? Where is the scholar? Where is the philosopher of this age? Has not God made foolish the wisdom of the world? For since in the wisdom of God the world through its wisdom did not know him, God was pleased through the foolishness of what was preached to save those who believe. Jews demand miraculous signs and Greeks look for wisdom, but we preach Christ crucified: a stumbling block to Jews and foolishness to Gentiles, but to those whom God has called, both Jews and Greeks, Christ the power of God and the wisdom of God. For the foolishness of God is wiser than man's wisdom, and the weakness of God is stronger than man's strength."

Consider a mind and heart without Christ; a mind and heart only capable of a higher power; a mind and heart that generalizes the magnificent, all-knowing God and rejects His son, Jesus Christ. Lost, yet in the futile attempts of their complicated minds, they point others to a wide road that leads to eternal damnation. REMEMBER: "Whoever has the Gold makes the Rules". God gave us His best when He gave us His son, Jesus Christ. It is God alone who makes the rules. The Bible still says that Jesus is the Way, the Truth, and the Life that redeems us to God; a God who administers grace, forgiveness, and restoration.

🐌 🐌 🐌 🐌 🐌

Have you commissioned yourself as a wise counselor using the temporal standards of the world instead of the eternal standards of God through faith in Jesus Christ? . . . Romans, chapter 1, verses 16—17, reads like this: "I am not ashamed of the gospel, because it is the power of God for the salvation of everyone who believes: first for the Jew, then for the Gentile. For in the gospel a righteousness from God is revealed, a righteousness that is by faith from first to last, just as it is written: 'the righteous will live by faith.'"

A Worldly Pep Talk

L ook at the similarities Dennis! . . . Don't be critical of
the differences! . . . Learn to work your own program!
. . . Get in touch with your feelings! . . . I call this a
departing pep talk. It's the same type of pep talk a football
team would hear after spending weeks in vigorous training
with repetitious plays, exercises, and memorizing offensive
and defensive plays designed to confuse and overcome their
opponent.

I had heard this pep talk before. It either came at the conclusion of my stay at a drug and alcohol treatment center or
was administered periodically, during that stay, with various
types of profanity at the daily meetings designed to enhance
my desire to beat my daily addiction to crack cocaine.

One of the key factors in winning a football game is mixing up plays. I never could imagine a team winning a game
using the same play every time, whether it be on the 20 yard
line or one foot from the goal line. I mean, after all, you
would think the defense would get wise after the same play-
er ended up with the ball on the same spot on the field and
ran the identical route over and over again. Not so! The
opponent continues to score using this same strategy.
Wouldn't you say it's time for a new strategy? Nope! You've
got to go along with the strategy and game plan that people
will accept and cheer for; the strategy and game plan that will

find the unsaved man in hell for eternity. And the saved man? Well, after all, it is the 20th century and this modern treatment that's been around for less than 30 years is more acceptable than a program that has been around since the beginning of time—even before the beginning of time, in eternity, and will be around after the end of time on into eternity.

What is the deity of Christ? Is it a modern way of thinking, with psychology as a backup, that aides the grace that Christ has offered us through Calvary? There has been a rash of new sin cropping up in the last 30 years: the new age, homosexuality, drunkenness, addiction to the ungodly, ruining our bodily temples, or learning to let feelings dictate our obedience; obedience to standards that were founded by people who lack a personal relationship with the answer to all of the human corruption. Perhaps we need a time machine so that we can go back to Sodom and Gomorrah to find out how new this age of sin really is. There will be millions who won't need a time machine because they will be able to ask, in person, the residents of hell who lived in the great cities of Sodom and Gomorrah.

I was hit with the words, "Although everything in scripture is true, not everything true is in scripture." That seems to be an honest statement in the context that this table I am using to write at and this chair I am sitting on are not in scripture. However, the context in which the words were used were in favor of using psychology along with scripture. One would wonder why a psychologist or psychiatrist, who is a professing Christian, would discount the authority or the completeness of God's Word when dealing with human problems. If we look at what the Bible says, we find out exactly how demonic and perverted it is to even question whether everything true for counsel can be found in scripture.

I suppose if I spent $90,000 on a new Mercedes, I would like to drive it. The degrees; the Bachelor's, the Master's, or Doctorate's in Psychology or related fields of study, deal specifically with the innermost thoughts of man and cost a fortune to obtain; not to mention the time involved. I know of an investment made for us at a cross. The time, wisdom, and price that went into Calvary is not to be discounted. Jesus did tell us in John, chapter 14, verse 6 that He is the Way, the Truth, and the Life. From Genesis, chapter 3 to the last chapter of Revelation, God's Word tells us that Jesus is *The Only Way, The Only Truth*, and *The Only Life*. We find the psychologist and psychiatrist using methods and wisdom as the standard. Intermittent scripture is then used as the out of context backup to the heathenistic distortion of God's grace through faith in Jesus Christ. Look at the other cults who believed that not everything that is true is in scripture. We can even go back to an entire nation of people who followed a cloud by day and a pillar of fire by night. They drank water from a rock that produced enough H_2O to quench the thirst of thousands, as well as all of their livestock. Previous to all of this, they witnessed their freedom from bondage as a result of plagues that never touched them. They walked through a parted sea and watched an entire army destroyed by the hand of the same loving God who would protect them, deliver them, and feed them from heaven.

Although all of this was true, God's chosen people still felt they needed more, so they made themselves a golden calf. Do you remember Aaron's reaction, found in Exodus, chapter 32, verse 5? "When Aaron saw this, he built an altar in front of the calf and announced, 'Tomorrow there will be a festival to the Lord.'" In the preceding verses, Aaron had originally answered the complaints of the people with the building of this idol. Aaron collected the gold and organized the show. His remorse for this sinful and hideous act of idolatry is also expressed in Exodus, chapter 32, verse 5. Aaron had a whole nation of people who accepted this idol and he tried to pacify his Lord and his conscience by building an altar at the feet of this alternative to God's grace. The golden calf wasn't in scripture until it was constructed. It became true to form as man's way of adding to, or replacing, the great God who gave us His son. Not only is there nothing new about the sin of today, there's also nothing different about the alternative.

In the futility of the human mind, we have found alternatives—rather than accepting the completeness of knowing the divine power of God through faith in Jesus Christ. It was true in the beginning and it will be true until Jesus returns. Eve wanted to become wiser and know her God through a deceptive, destructive, disobedient method—so she took hold of sin and found she had been deceived. I can hear it now, "God, my professor of psychology and this teacher gave me the information and told me to add to your Word and use your name to promote this perversion of grace." Hebrews, chapter 10, verses 28—39 defines the perversion of grace. It reads like this: "Anyone who rejects the law of Moses died without mercy on the testimony of two or three witnesses. How much more severely do you think a man deserves to be punished who has trampled the Son of God underfoot, who has treated as an unholy thing the blood of the covenant that sanctified him, and who has insulted the Spirit of grace? For we know him who said, 'It is mine to avenge; I will repay,' and again, 'The Lord will judge his people.' It is a dreadful thing to fall into the hands of the living God. Remember those earlier days after you had received the light, when you stood your ground in a great contest in the face of suffering. Sometimes you were publicly exposed to insult and persecution; at other times you stood side by side with those who were so treated. You sympathized with those in prison and joyfully accepted the confiscation of your property, because you knew that you yourself had better and lasting possessions. So do not throw away your confidence; it will be richly rewarded. You need to persevere so that when you have done the will of God, you will receive what he has promised. For in just a very little while, 'He who is coming will come and will not delay. But my righteous one will live by faith. And if he shrinks back, I will not be pleased with him.' But we are not of those who

"Look at the similarities Dennis! . . . Don't be critical of the differences! . . . Learn to work your own program! . . . Get in touch with your feelings!"

shrink back and are destroyed, but of those who believe and are saved."

"Look at the similarities Dennis! Don't be critical of the differences!" Remember the opening statement in this chapter? These words are the standard introduction to the worldly pep talk.

Suppose I was a plain-clothes police officer and I went out and bought a brand new revolver. I holstered my weapon and began to make my rounds. A call comes over my radio that there is an armed robbery in progress. So, I turn on my lights and siren, that are concealed behind the grill of my patrol car, and I am off to the scene of the crime. I find myself confronted by a very angry man. I pull out my new service revolver and fire a warning shot over his head. The criminal returns fire and bullets are bouncing off my patrol car like popcorn. I fire a burst of rounds at the suspect and he is still standing. "I am a marksman! Why didn't I drop him? I missed!" . . . I wake up in the hospital paralyzed from gunshot wounds. I have lost the use of my legs. I don't understand! I face regret. I reminisce in my mind over and over again the series of events that have taken place. I have never missed! I am a marksman! I always hit what I shoot at! My chief shows up and there are tears in his eyes. My family is next to him and they are shaking their heads and they too are crying. "Why?" they ask me. "Why would you take a pistol on duty with you that is only good for starting races?" "What are you talking about? I paid good money for that pistol!" is my response. "It's a replica; an imitation. It wasn't made or designed to fire live ammunition," my chief answers. With the agony of a new cripple, I reply, "I don't understand. The man who sold it to me . . . I . . . I . . . Oh dear God, I never test fired it. It looked and felt like the one I always wanted."

There are many counterfeits and replicas for godliness. To test fire and discern what is of God and what is not: (1) Read your Bible daily, (2) Pray regularly, (3) Faithfully attend a church that teaches of unconditional forgiveness through faith in Jesus Christ. First John, chapter 4, verses 1—6 is a test firing from God's Word and is directed at worldly pep talks. It reads like this: "Dear friends, do not believe every spirit, but test the spirits to see whether they are from God, because many false prophets have gone out into the world. This is how you can recognize the Spirit of God: Every spirit that acknowledges that Jesus Christ has come in the flesh is from God, but every spirit that does not acknowledge Jesus is not from God. This is the spirit of the antichrist, which you have heard is coming and even now is already in the world. You dear children, are from God and have overcome them, because the one who is in you is greater than the one who is in the world. They are from the world and therefore speak from the viewpoint of the world, and the world listens to them. We are from God, and whoever knows God listens to us; but whoever is not from God does not listen to us. This is how we recognize the Spirit of truth and the spirit of falsehood."

Let's take a look at the second encouragement from the worldly pep talk. "Learn to work your own program!" Personally, I was never sure what my program was. It kept changing with circumstances. If I had been smart enough to handle my own life, I wouldn't have spent the years I did in my misery as well as in the misery of others. The same treatment centers that told me my best thinking got me into trouble were now telling me to work my own program. I realize today that any program, counselor, treatment center, clergy, or friend that eliminates the deity of Christ, or waters it down, is described in I John, chapter 4, verses 1 through 6 as the spirit of the antichrist and should have no part in the Christian life. I look back on the numerous treatment centers, counselors, family members, and even some church leaders who stressed consistency in my life, yet their programs, counsel, and theories were inconsistent with scripture. My family was gone because of my inconsistency in Christ; the same family that told me at the entrance to one treatment center that this was a case of where "the end justifies the means". I was confronted at an intervention by relatives and they openly shared all the bad things I had done over the years. I look back at the inconsistencies in that intervention. For instance, one relative in the circle was an ex-drug dealer who had given me my first line of cocaine. He was also the same person who, a few years later, would counsel my wife to divorce me.

Someday the eastern sky will split wide open and we will see Jesus. This will be the final result of the grace of our loving God; the result of a tragedy expressed by Jesus' suffering at the cross. The eternal tragedies will be the professing Christians who, through word or deed, conveyed that what Jesus did at Calvary wasn't enough. I suppose one could try to express how they felt by saying that "the end justifies the means". The scripture found in James, chapter 4, verses 4—12 doesn't tell us to get wiser, it warns us to wise up. For those of you who still believe that interventions and the worldly way are proper, and are judging situations and people's sin through the eyes of man instead of through the eyes of Christ, read James, chapter 4, verses 4—12. It reads like this: "You adulterous people, don't you know that friendship with the world is hatred toward God? Anyone who chooses to be a friend of the world becomes an enemy of God. Or do you think Scripture says without reason that the spirit he caused to live in us envies intensely? But he gives us more grace. That is why Scripture says: 'God opposes the proud but gives grace to the humble.' Submit yourselves, then to God. Resist the devil, and he will flee from you. Come near to God and he will come near to you. Wash your hands, you sinners, and purify your hearts, you double-minded. Grieve, mourn and wail. Change your laughter to mourning and your joy to gloom. Humble yourselves before the Lord, and he will lift you up. Brothers, do not slander one another. Anyone who speaks against his brother or judges him speaks against the law and judges it. When you judge the law, you are not keeping it, but sitting in judgment on it. There is only one Lawgiver and Judge, the one who is able to save and destroy. But you—who are you to judge your neighbor?"

"Get in touch with your feelings!" This will be the final and most blasphemous, damaging, and camouflaged discouragement to the obedient spirit of the Born Again believer in Jesus Christ. Feelings can only feel. Feelings have been the playground for the demonic influence in the heart of humans since the first sin. The Christian's obedience isn't contingent upon his or her feelings. Our obedience is based on God's Word and submission to the Lord's will. Jesus got in touch with His feelings and expressed humanly the grief and anguish of His upcoming torture. If ever a man had feelings that rooted deep and tore Him apart inside, it was Jesus. He was all man and all God. The fact that He was all God let Him see His future. The undescribable feelings that were felt by Jesus because He was all man are expressed in scripture. Matthew, chapter 26, verses 38 and 39 reads like this: "Then he said to them, 'My soul is overwhelmed with sorrow to the point of death. Stay here and keep watch with me.' Going a little farther, he fell with his face to the ground and prayed, 'My Father, if it is possible, may this cup be taken from me. Yet not as I will, but as you will.'" In Gethsemane, Jesus got in touch with His feelings and became obedient in spite of them. The word *Gethsemane* means "oil press", a place for squeezing the oil from olives. How beautiful a thought—that the obedience to His father was the essence of His love for sinners. A love that, in a few hours after Gethsemane, would press the Savior to unexplainable pain; a love that would show, as clear and as pure as olive oil, the redemption for you and me.

               ❧   ❧   ❧   ❧   ❧

Matthew, chapter 16, verse 24: "Then Jesus said to his disciples, 'If anyone would come after me, he must deny himself and take up his cross and follow me.'" Is Jesus asking us to respond to our feelings or to respond to our obedience and total commitment and follow Him?

We sit in church and sing how we strive to be like Jesus and then we pulverize, distort, and insult the Spirit of grace by relying on human counsel based on human wisdom. Our legal system today is riddled with Christian divorce cases where families are victims of the ungodly counsel from treatment centers, lawyers, clergy, psychiatrists, psychologists, and well-read, home-grown, do-it-yourselfers who hammer legalism at people in the name of God. The truth in all of this is that the many variables and approaches of ungodly counsel are subtle and usually take a long time to manifest themselves in a church or in the mind of the individual Christian. When the cancer called deception and distortion—or sometimes, just plain blatant disobedience to God's Word—takes root in the heart and mind of church leadership, we witness the result of unscripturally based counsel. When the leadership looks to the world for direction instead of the *Word*, we find a parallel in II Timothy, chapter 4, verses 1—5 like this: "In the presence of God and of Christ Jesus, who will judge the living and the dead, and in view of his appearing and his kingdom, I give you this charge: Preach the Word; be prepared in season and out of season; correct, rebuke and encourage—with great patience and careful instruction. For the time will come when men will not put up with sound doctrine. Instead, to suit their own desires, they will gather around them a great number of teachers to say what their itching ears want to hear. They will turn their ears away from the truth and turn aside to myths. But you, keep your head in all situations, endure hardship, do the work of an evangelist, discharge all the duties of your ministry."

For the man or woman who discounts, distorts, compromises, or questions—in word or deed—the completeness of scripture for any or all of our needs: I Corinthians, chapter 2, verses 13—16 says this: "This is what we speak, not in words taught us by human wisdom but in words taught by the Spirit, expressing spiritual truths in spiritual words. The man without the Spirit does not accept the things that come from the Spirit of God, for they are foolishness to him, and he cannot understand them, because they are spiritually discerned. The spiritual man makes judgments about all things but he himself is not subject to any man's judgment: 'For who has known the mind of the Lord that he may instruct Him?' But we have the mind of Christ."

I'll complete this chapter with the same question and statement the apostle Paul asked of, and made to, the church in Corinth. "For who has known the mind of the Lord that he may instruct him? But we have the mind of Christ."

CHAPTER 11

A Victim or a Survivor?

There is always curiosity inside me when I'm leading a seminar, speaking to a congregation, or just plain one on one counseling. I sometimes wonder how people see me; specifically the silent ones. I hope with all of my heart that they are being impacted for the glory of Jesus Christ. I have received many compliments as a speaker, teacher, etc., but always wonder how those with empathy see me. It seems lately my harshest critics are those who say they can relate to my past, not because they have been there themselves, but because a friend or relative they have spent a large amount of time around has been there. They seem to have a variety of opinions and have made it clear that those opinions are of God. I have found not even a hint of biblical fact to support their notions. Yes, one of their relatives or friends has been through similar circumstances and therefore my critiquors seem to be more interested in making a point than seeking the truth for themselves from God's Word. Some of these critiquors are in high places of authority in some sort of ministry. I even received one letter twice. The exact same letter. It was important to this individual that their message got through.

Whenever I listen to people's personal testimonies, I ask myself this: *1st* Does it line up with scripture?, *2nd* Does it endorse religion or a relationship to Christ?, *3rd* Is the infor-

103

mation first hand or does it have the makings of passed on information not found in the Bible?

It seems that preconceived judgements, or building one's defense for such behavior, is very important to the administrator. For example: we get our ears tickled a little bit so that the administrator of the critiques can undermine our personal testimony. I have found this more so when people are trying to undermine the scriptures, prayer, Bible study, fellowship, and servanthood as "not enough to overcome one's past". I have been criticized for presenting the plan of salvation in a seminar titled "Loving Others". I was told it was not part of the curriculum. The fact that the seminar was in a prison and the plan of salvation presentation took 3 1/2 minutes out of the 8 1/2 hours meant very little to my critiquor who was there to evaluate my performance. I started to mention the Holy Spirit's leading in rebuttal to a written evaluation I had received. To which I was told, "If it's not planned and doesn't fit, don't use it!" Another comment was made over the same incident by someone who relied on passed on information and wasn't there to hear the content or context of what I had presented and had this to say: "You are not there to win converts." I suppose I should have made it clear that when you employ Dennis Tinsman to lead any seminar, or speak in any environment, I will present my Lord in the way He expects me to. In season and out of season, planned or not planned. That's because the plan of salvation is the most important curriculum ever written. Romans, chapter 1, verse 16 reads: "I am not ashamed of the gospel, because it is the power of God for the salvation of everyone who believes: first for the Jew, then for the Gentile." As far as the specifics of the plan of salvation in a "Loving Others" seminar, John, chapter 15, verses 12—13 couldn't say it any better: "My command is this: Love each other as I have loved you. Greater love has no one than this, that he lay down his life for his friends."

You see, Mr. or Mrs. Critiquor, I look at myself as a survivor and not a victim. This chapter was not titled by me. It was titled by Mr. Richard Hole. Richard Hole is serving 20 years in the state penitentiary in Muskegon, Michigan for a crime that I hate. I hate the crime, but through the plan of salvation, and seeing people through the eyes of Christ, I've learned to love the criminal. I want you to read Richard's testimony just the way I received it. Perhaps you will see, Mr. or Mrs. Critiquor, just why the plan of salvation is so important in a "Loving Others" seminar. Perhaps, Mr. or Mrs. Critiquor, you will see why the plan of salvation is so important to an ex-convict like myself and a convict like Mr. Richard Hole.

The following is the word for word testimony of Mr. Richard Hole, written by Mr. Richard Hole.

My name is Rick. It's a Sunday evening and I am sitting in my room at my typewriter. My roommate is watching TV. Earlier today at our Evening Service, I spoke with Dennis— he was here on a return trip after doing a Prison Fellowship weekend seminar two months ago. Dennis is the type who, when you spend one of those weekends together, it seems like you have known forever.

During the last month something unique and inspiring has happened to me. Dennis, as a survivor of sexual assault as a child, could relate to this. You see, I am serving a 20 year bit for the same thing, involving my nephew Dave, who was nine years old at the time. I have 8 1/2 of those years completed.

During the seminar, Dennis related some of how he felt as a survivor, and I wanted to ask him just how much he had been able to forgive the perpetrator. But I couldn't open up enough. I'd seen too many victims on TV talk shows full of pain, hate, and a desire for revenge. Somehow Dennis seemed more of a survivor than a victim.

I had, all in all, a good childhood. We never had much, but we always got by. My dad did unskilled labor, and recessions in the 50's and 60's always hit us hard. But we always ate well, and learned that home-made bread was by far the best. And we had enough clothes, and mom kept us clean. Dad was there as a Cub and Boy Scout leader and we did a lot together. For pocket money, there were lawns to mow, bottles to collect.

I did well in school. Science was my favorite, along with band. We were a church family. At age 8 I was baptized. I understood what that meant and took it seriously, and continued believing in Jesus as my Savior all these years.

In high school I got interested in electronics, radios, and computers. That became my life's vocation: a great scholarship package at Michigan Tech and a degree after four years.

Somewhere in those years I began to take a warp in sexual activity. There was a young neighbor from a broken home, starved for attention and affection, and I drifted to some very inappropriate touching. Over the next ten years or so, it was the same with a dozen or more other victims. And like a dam with a small leak, erosion soon sets in. The leak becomes a torrent. What I did to those victims, all of them youngsters who trusted and loved me, became worse and worse, crossing the lines between 4th, 3rd, and 1st degree criminal offenses.

All the time I deceived myself that as long as the kids were willing and returning again, it just couldn't be all that seriously bad. Less and less often my conscience would bother me and I would find the need to confess to the Lord and be forgiven. Ah, the difference between confession and repentance—I didn't make that difference. And I could do pretty well with self-control. After all, I once went for two whole years clean.

My last victim was my nephew Dave. It was Thanksgiving and my family had gathered at my new house for the day. My life was going well—a great job at the local college teaching electronics. A great place out in the woods. Active in the church choir. Regular volunteer in the college hockey press box. I was active in several civic organizations and almost too busy to get in trouble.

But not busy enough. Young Dave was fascinated by some of my "toys", and stayed for the weekend. And it was the same thing over again. It was the same thing over again several times over the next few months. Until one day he slipped a word that exposed me and my evil side. A few days later I found myself in the clutches of the criminal justice system.

There are easier things in life than being a child molester in prison. You have to learn to keep your mouth shut. To choose friends carefully. And to learn that the "system" cares nothing at all about rehabilitation. You have to do for yourself. And a big part of that is to find the right "crutch."

For years I was dedicated to the Lord. Well, mostly dedicated — 95% dedicated. That's an "A" in any exam! If you take a pie and cut out 5%, you'll hardly notice anything missing. But 5% not dedicated to the Lord is like being 5% cancerous. You are in BIG trouble. That 5% I left for myself kept growing. Like that trickle of water breaching the dam until it finally breaks.

My life broke wide open and I hit bottom hard. But with the only true rehabilitation, God's own healing, my uphill battle is well under way.

It was one month ago. I returned to my room from work and got ready for the expected visit from my parents. They show up here regularly. But that night they did not show up, and that's reason to call to see if there is any emergency. Much later that night I finally got to make my phone call.

They hadn't come that day because they had received a phone call from Dave. Our first contact in nine years. He was about to turn 18 years old, and said he wanted, more than anything, for his birthday to come and see me. Would I be willing? And when was the very first possible day he could do it?

So they arranged to meet him later that week. I must have had a thousand conversations inside my mind. What would I say to him? Would I be able to look him in the eye? It took two nights of tossing before the next good night's sleep. On the appointed day, as I sat in the visiting room waiting, my nerves were in a knot. Could I keep from becoming sick right there in front of everyone? I wasn't sure whether I felt like I was waiting for Christmas morning—or waiting for a firing squad.

The door opened and he stepped inside. We spent several hours getting re-acquainted. This young man was all smiles, ear to ear. Graduating at the top of his class, ready to start at a top-rate Christian college this fall. I wanted to make sure he knew I held nothing against him, I had nothing to forgive him for—he was the victim. I wanted to explode the misconceptions he might have about the quality of life I have in prison—movies and media give a view that accentuates the violent and bizarre, when the reality is a lot closer to endless boredom punctuated by an occasional moment when something interesting happens. It was a blessing to see him happy.

That day I learned something about forgiveness. something you can't learn by reading about it. Not a lip-service of forgiveness, not a gentlemen's agreement to overlook an offense, not even something that can be expressed in words. But I felt forgiveness. When Jesus says, "I forgive you," it must be that sort of forgiveness.

I think Dave is not a victim—he is a survivor. I wonder about the others, which are they? What trail of damage did I leave in their lives. Have they overcome it, or does it haunt them? One day there will be answers. But what about me— am I a victim or a survivor? I don't have to be a victim of my past. I can be a survivor.

ॐ ॐ ॐ ॐ ॐ

Picking up after our yesterdays, trying to make a today count for something, and looking for hope to face tomorrow—with its sin and the inflicted results of a past—is impossible. Impossible, that is, without Christ. One of the greatest promises ever written is found in Isaiah, chapter 43, verses 1,2, and 3. This promise has been made possible by Jesus Christ through his magnificent, eternal, and incomparable plan of salvation.

"Fear not, for I have redeemed
you;
I have summoned you by name;
you are mine.
When you pass through the waters,
I will be with you;
and when you pass through the rivers,
they will not sweep over you.
When you walk through the fire,
you will not be burned;
the flames will not set you
ablaze.
For I am the Lord, your God,
the Holy One of Israel, your Savior; . . ."

CHAPTER 12

Those Barking Dogs

A few years ago, I parked my prodigal lifestyle. For those of you who don't understand the term "prodigal lifestyle" . . . it's the lifestyle of a Christian that has everyone believing that the person in question is anything but a Christian. A re-dedication to the Lord has its good points. One major point for me was: I quit living in my own man-made, self-inflicted hell. I began realizing shortly thereafter that other people were able to inflict just as much hurt and hardship.

I marvel at Jesus' response to Pontius Pilate in the Gospel of John, chapter 19, verse 11 that reads: "Jesus answered, 'You would have no power over me if it were not given to you from above. Therefore the one who handed me over to you is guilty of a greater sin.'" We read in the preceding verses that Jesus spoke of His eternal kingdom, while Pilate was addressing the temporal kingdom. John, chapter 18, verses 33—37, reads like this: "Pilate then went back inside the palace, summoned Jesus and asked him, 'Are you the king of the Jews?'

'Is that your own idea,' Jesus asked, 'or did others talk to you about me?'

'Am I a Jew?' Pilate replied. 'It was your people and your chief priests who handed you over to me. What is it you have done?'

Jesus said, 'My kingdom is not of this world. If it were, my servants would fight to prevent my arrest by the Jews. But now my kingdom is from another place.'

'You are a king, then!' said Pilate.

Jesus answered, 'You are right in saying I am a king. In fact, for this reason I was born, and for this I came into the world, to testify to the truth. Everyone on the side of truth listens to me.'"

Mr. Pontius Pilate sums up his dilemma in the opening words to verse 38 in John, chapter 18. Pilate addresses the Son of God in private and out of earshot of the embittered crowd—which was bent on destroying an innocent man— with the question, "What is truth?" I suppose if the Governor of Judah, who is known to us as Pontius Pilate, would have perceived the outcome of the man who stood before him for sentencing, it would have still made little difference. If Governor Pilate had the benefit of New Testament scripture, Old Testament prophecy, and several other accounts of Jesus' life—thus making the current events of that day a soon to be historical fact—it probably would have made little difference as the governor faced the out of control crowd. I suppose I base that statement on the actions of our own government in America and its so-called system of checks and balances—and the leader or leaders who face the numerous citizens that are just as out of control. Listening to the shouts of immoral and ungodly people literally caused the death of Jesus. Fortunately, Jesus is eternal. However, I have yet to read of any government that is anything but temporal.

A few years ago, the Reverend Ned Graham told me, in a very direct way, "Stop listening to barking dogs." I know he could tell how bothered I was. The simple truth was that I started basing my self-worth on the fact that I was unable to pay my child support. The amount was way beyond any means I had, or ever have had, to accumulate that amount of money. Relatives and some old church friends treated me as an outcast. When my ex-wife married a very close friend of mine from my old hometown church, and some of my immediate family attended along with another very close friend—whom I had held several confidences in—I was crushed. The hope for reconciliation with my wife was gone. I felt that both my focus on the ministry and my relationship to Christ were dwindling. My conclusion from these devastating circumstances was that in a matter of days after the wedding I would be stripped and left without anything, including all hope, to go on.

My mind started going over and over those nasty and seemingly uncontrollable "What ifs?". My thoughts were once again consumed with that age old game of "Who's to blame?" The questions raced into my mind at rapid-fire speed. Is this God's payback for all the tragedies I had inflicted on others through my more than reckless past? What about my unloyal family and friends? When do they get theirs for all their un-Christlike actions? I found myself becoming more and more consumed with those thoughts and it was showing up in my eyes and attitude. I remained faithful to my Bible reading and prayer and literally forced myself to stay in Christian service. Amidst all the turmoil, I felt this subtle voice inside me that was saying, "And this too will pass, Dennis."

I went to my pastor who had bottle fed me spiritually until I was able to get on my feet. He had stood beside me in Jesus' name and, at times, encouraged me to seek answers through studying the Bible—not from him. In short, he nurtured me and tactfully told me that Jesus wants me to walk. I guess he wanted me to tap into the Holy Spirit instead of always running to him. He taught me, through his example, that sometimes we must stand alone, and *stand* we must.

I looked at Pastor and began to spill my guts. I recall him telling me a few months before that sometimes it's best to jump right in the middle of your troubles and kick your way out. This had been new ground for me. I had spent most of my past years burying tragedies and digging them up over and over again in my mind. They became so much a part of me that I was afraid to let go of them. I couldn't imagine what it would be like to come to Jesus with a full load of burdens and walk away with empty hands. After dumping my thoughts on Pastor for about half of an hour, he startled me with his response. Here I am, deep in hurt, haven't slept good for weeks, and he sums up his counsel in one sentence. In his boisterous voice, he stated, "The dogs bark, Dennis, but the caravan moves on!" I know that wasn't one of his original lines, but the application was perfect and I expanded on it. It was more than ironic that I had received the same counsel almost three years prior from the Reverend Ned Graham over lunch.

Being in the ministry is a tough road. Even if you're on that narrow road, the trials can become distractions that sometimes lead us on mental wild goose chases that slow up our performance, hinder our ministries, and (in some tragic situations) the mental bondage, if not brought to the surface, may drive out the high level of commitment a person has when he is sold out to Jesus.

The application of "those barking dogs" is very personal to me. I know of a particular situation that happened to a young boy who had just started serving the early morning newspaper in his neighborhood. I am able to relate well to this situation because I was that young boy.

After several weeks of learning my paper route and being introduced to my customers, I was ready to set out on my own. My first morning on the job as a full-fledged employee was exciting. I had worked hard in training and I knew my route like my own backyard. I was assured in my mind that I was on the threshold of financial prosperity. I approached my first customer's house and tossed my first newspaper end over end. Yes! A direct hit! I loved baseball and I was a pitcher. This made me a natural for throwing the rolled-up, rubber-banded papers numerous feet and making a direct hit. About halfway through my route, a beast of nature appeared. A teeth bearing, hair standing up on the back, growling beast of nature—and he was blocking by path. "Wait a minute," I thought to myself, "this is Bernard. I remember this mongrel as being a hand-licking, tail-wagging boy's best friend. Why just yesterday, and every day of my training period, this mutt had been friendly to the kid who had the route before me. Bernard was his buddy and he had acted like he was my buddy for the past few weeks. The old paper boy shared with me how he looked forward to Bernard's pleasant licks and cuddles. Bernard had been an absolute gem. In an effort to calm him down, I called his name, "Bernard, it's me. Remember me? I'm the boy who has scratched your ears, kissed your head, and talked baby talk to you." The kid who had the paper route before was a few years older than me—and when we would stop to pet Bernard, he'd look at me like I was some sort of weirdo kid as I kissed this mutt and talked to him in my unique high-pitched voice. "Bernard!" I said abruptly. Unfortunately, Bernard realized that he could intimidate me and so—he did. For the next six months, I went about four or five blocks out of my way to avoid Bernard. I tested the pooch a couple of times at about two week intervals. That dog knew what time I was coming and he sat in his yard waiting for me. I'd call his name but it was the same old thing. I figured that in the first six months of my paper route, Bernard had cost me 20 minutes a day, 2 hours and 20 minutes a week, 9 hours and 20 minutes a month; and I had wasted a grand total of 2 days and 8 hours on a hair bag.

This was my paper route and I was getting fed up. I wanted to seek wise counsel, but who does a twelve year old boy turn to; to solve this . . . this doggie dilemma?

I was sitting on the front porch of our house one Saturday. I remember it being Saturday because I wasn't in school. I was sitting there talking to Ludwig Von Beethoven. We all know that Ludwig Von Beethoven, the composer, is dead. We had a wiener dog that was not your average dachshund. We had always kept him inside around noon-time because that's when the mailman made his rounds. Ludwig was very bold. He did have one thing in common with Mr. Beethoven, the composer. He was deaf. Not deaf all of the time, just when he was in pursuit of Mr. Mailman. Ludwig flew out of my arms and before I could grab him he was in a dead run toward Mr. Mailman. Mr. Mailman froze and I watched as his hand disappeared into his pouch. In the twinkling of an eye, his hand came out of his pouch in a fist and as he opened his hand he emitted a white powdery cloud a few feet in front of himself. As our little wiener dog entered the cloud, his speed was almost instantly reduced to a crawl. I watched as Ludwig stopped and began sneezing and shaking his head relentlessly. This frothing at the mouth little wiener dog had been reduced to a grovelling, powerless, ha-choo! ha-choo!

I walked off our porch, went down, picked Ludwig up, carried him inside, and returned to pick up our mail. The mailman stated in a gruff voice, "If you want your mail son, you'd better keep your dog inside when I'm in the neighborhood." I told him I was sorry, but other things were on my mind. You guessed it—Bernard. "What is that stuff?" was my inquiry to Mr. Mailman. "It's my own little recipe," he replied. I spent the next few minutes explaining to him my problem with Bernard. Mr. Mailman's attitude changed and he agreed to give me his secret recipe. "Now listen, sonny," he began, "you take three parts pepper and one part flour." . . . "Yeah, and ?" was my more than inquisitive attitude. I was waiting for the rest of the recipe when Mr. Mailman stated, "That's it!" "That's it?" I questioned. "Yep! That's it," he reassured me. Mr. Mailman told me he always carried a rock in his pocket in case his concoction of pepper and flour wasn't quite enough.

I spent the rest of my day and most of the evening daydreaming about ending a problem that had consumed me for months . . . and I could hardly wait. Everything I needed was found in every American kitchen. I had six months of anger, frustration, intimidation, and even some bitterness toward

Bernard, all of which had festered into more than just gaining back 20 minutes a day. I wanted to get even. I flew out of bed that morning, which in and of itself was a miracle, got dressed, raced downstairs, loaded up my papers, filled a small pouch with the black speckled flour and I was off. I had to travel about five minutes to get to the beginning of my paper route and I found me a nice big rock on the way. Now my adrenaline was pumping. At each house I delivered, I anticipated my confrontation with Bernard. I was becoming a mad dog myself as I plotted how I would use this rock on old Bernard whether he needed it or not.

I began going up the street that Bernard lived on and I was ready to flour, pepper, and rock this dingo into oblivion. I could tell old Bernard was a little bit surprised when I crossed the point of no return. I approached him with a handful of this burning hot flour cloud and, in my other hand, the rock to finish him off. Old Bernard began to growl and his hair stood up. I walked up about five feet from him, stopped, and yelled, "Come on!" Bernard quit growling and just looked at me. I walked up to him and he laid down immediately and looked up at me. I spoke a little less seriously, "Come on you mutt, this is the day of reckoning." Bernard rolled over and gave me a look of solemn gentleness. "What in the world's going on here?" I thought to myself. I bent down, took my hand off my rock, and dusted the flour and pepper mixture off my hand. I sat there for about two or three minutes yelling at Bernard. He kept looking at me with those eyes of love. I reached out with my hand. My voice turned from yelling to talking and I began to scratch his belly. His hind leg began to move up and down as if it were on a hinge.

The weeks and months that followed, Bernard and I grew quite close. I spent at least twenty minutes visiting with Bernard each morning. I talked with Ludwig in that stupid baby voice of mine that I use to talk to dogs—and I'm sure Ludwig approved of me taking some of his doggie biscuits to Bernard. Up until now, I never shared my experience that I'd had with Bernard with anyone. Ludwig knew only because it was his doggie biscuits I was sharing.

I think one of the most crushing moments for me in those years was the morning I went up Bernard's street and he wasn't there. As I rounded the corner after serving my papers on his street, . . . well, there lay Bernard on the side of the road. I took my newspaper sack off my shoulder and laid it underneath a tree and I carried Bernard around the corner to his owner.

Over the years, Bernard (and my relationship to this hound of hinderance) had been stuffed way back in the archives of my mind. Today I think about how much time I wasted on a noise- making, tough-looking mongrel who ended up being my friend anyway. I suppose one might derive that lesson to be important -and it is. But it only parallels another lesson that is much more important.

Several years ago, I was introduced to a man who became a very dear friend. In fact, He's the best friend I've ever had. After a long introduction, He made me feel good and showed me great affection. For whatever reason, I thought I could manipulate this friend and intimidate Him. I became an angry dog to this friend. He had a record of everything I had ever done against Him, and at a time when He could have destroyed me, He chose to forgive. While flat on my back spiritually, I was ready for an unconditional surrender. Instead of His wrath, I received His mercy. I had been a dog and had defiantly bitten the hand that died for me. It had always been so easy to remember other's canine actions and dismiss the ones I had. I now meet with my friend daily for at least twenty minutes. It has become the most important time of each day and I actually look forward to it. He sneaks me blessings from time to time. Blessings that belong to Him. I am pleasantly assured of something else. Someday I'll find myself at the side of that narrow road. My friend will stop, place my sins at the foot of a tree, and carry me just around the corner to my owner.

ॐ ॐ ॐ ॐ ॐ

Jesus said very little to the condemning ridicule, accusations, and shouts of an out of control crowd. He reacted to His accusers with love. He was obedient to the task at hand without resentments. It meant suffering! But in spite of extreme torturing distractions—physical, spiritual, and mental—He finished the plan laid out by His Heavenly Father. In the name of Jesus Christ, we are called to love *"Those Barking Dogs"*.

CHAPTER 13

A Wolf in Sheep's Clothing

Part I: The Over All Situation

What a mess we have in our church. What a mess. The wavering tone in his voice expressed deep anxiety. I had never seen him like this—nor could I have pictured him, before this, hurting so deeply. He seemed to keep the tear ducts in his eyes under control but as he faced me I could tell that he was all cried out. My old nature started bouncing around in my mind and I wanted to chop some ears off.

I remember a preacher telling me a couple years ago that Jesus had given His Christian followers the title of "sheep". He also informed me that pastors in both the Old and New Testament context were referred to as shepherds. Jesus being the "King Shepherd" relies on earthly shepherds, known as pastors, to lead a flock; a flock being a whole bunch of sheep. This particular preacher also told me that a sheep's diet consists of grass; grass being the Word of God. He concluded his brief lesson with the statement: "Sheep eat grass; they don't eat other sheep."

We had one that had risen in leadership within the church and, as such, we had us a wolf that was indeed eating sheep. As its diet shifted, this wolf began acting like the shepherd and like his immediate family may be a delicacy. After

watching our pastor react to the sin, I knew why he had been called to be a shepherd and why I was a sheep. Even if I had been able to get around the fact that I was divorced, through the various interpretations of Bible doctrine, I still realized (towards the end of the crisis) that God had me right where He wanted me.

Shepherds can always tell when a wolf has been in their flock. The wolves prowl and seem to latch on to the weak ones. At times the wolf appears to have the voice of a lamb, the insights of a counselor, and the needs of a servant. When put to the test, they utter sounds that are inconsistent with a sheep's vocabulary. For instance, one sound they make goes something like this: "If I leave, I'm gonna take several with me." A wolf will point out flaws in the flock and its shepherd. They are creatures of manipulative gossip that camouflage their beastly nature. This scenario also allows them to cloak outburst and false accusations. Confidences that were once shared become vindictive ridicule.

When I was in seminary, I recall a guest speaker we had who had been a sheep farmer turned preacher. He still had several of the wooly critters and was quick to point our their weaknesses. I remember one comment that he made went something like this: "We don't have to be concerned where the wolf's been. We can all see where the wolf has been. If I'm a pastor, I want to know where the wolf's going."

It's interesting to see how disloyal sheep can be to real loyalty. Loyalty isn't always followed by popularity, but it certainly speaks the truth in all things. Real loyalty is the by-product of perseverance and servanthood. Loyalties among sheep, as a shepherd has to learn, are few and far between. Everything in a sheep's worldly nature tells it to turn its back on the shepherd and follow a bellowing, manipulative wolf whose sole purpose is to satisfy its own desires and take away from the flock. I was intrigued, in a negative sort of way, as I watched the wolf's manipulative character turning the truth upside-down. As the wolf retreats from the flock, it may assume the title of "martyr" to cover its tracks. Wolves can be loners, may run in packs, and they can be males or females. Many of the disloyal sheep began to take on some of the characteristics of the wolf. Sheep who start to follow a wolf kind of become like the little wooden puppet who, in the Walt Disney movie *Pinocchio*, literally made a different character of himself. Those of you who may have seen the movie may recall that Pinocchio was saved in the nick of time by a conscience named Jiminy Cricket. However, there were many others who weren't so fortunate.

Proverbs, chapter 6, verses 16—19 gives God's perspective on sheep that have become the spiritual three course meal of a howling, manipulative wolf.

> "There are six things the Lord hates,
> seven that are detestable to him:
> haughty eyes,
> a lying tongue,
> hands that shed innocent blood,
> a heart that devises wicked schemes,
> feet that are quick to rush into evil,
> a false witness who pours out lies
> and a man who stirs up dissension among brothers."

Part II: A Lamb Being Led to the Slaughter

"Is there anything wrong?" she asked me. "I'm not quite sure," was my response. I went on to ask her more in depth, "Are all those pills for your headaches? How come your taking them at irregular intervals?" The prescription called for "as needed" and this young lady was doing just that.

This particular chapter has been one of the toughest things I've ever written. Tough because it hits real close to home. It would be easy to speculate and do some ear chopping. Perhaps this time on paper. I'll stick to the facts and the correlating scripture so you, as the reader, can assess the situation. One more thing before I continue, I've referred to ear chopping twice in this chapter. I am actually pointing to scripture found in the Gospel of John, chapter 18, verse 10 that reads: "Then Simon Peter, who had a sword, drew it and struck the high priest's servant, cutting off his right ear. (The servant's name was Malchus.)"

Simon Peter, who was one of the twelve disciples, was also a big, burly fisherman who went after ears with more than just a sword. When I refer to ear chopping by myself, well, I am still a little rough around the edges and have been known to look for a bigger hammer to deal with a seemingly out of control situation.

I'm serious when I tell you that this situation hits real close to home. I didn't know, when I confronted Carol about her pills, just how entangled a life can become when the counsel that is being administered is being administered by a critter who isn't making the sounds a sheep makes. As I continued to express my concerns for Carol's daily usage of pills, she became defensive. I began praying for Carol, and found myself in tears several times. About two weeks after my confrontation with Carol, she asked me one evening to sit down with her because she had something she wanted to share with me. I was hoping and praying that she would open up and talk to me about the pills. Well, I got my prayers answered—and confirmed even deeper some absolutes about the counsel given in Carol's past.

Three years before her introduction to the pills, Carol married her high school sweetheart. Unable to graduate because she was pregnant, Carol gave her sins to Jesus, received His grace, and also accepted the reality that there was a little baby on the way. Three years and two children later, Carol found herself in front of a counselor who also bore the title of Christian. Her high school sweetheart loved the bars, booze, and pornography. Like most men with the latter of the three sins, he treated Carol like a dishrag, was verbally and emotionally abusive, and had ended up using her as a punching bag. Reaching out for help, Carol was in the hindsight mode of "if only I had known". When Christians start dealing with their sin, it's always best to consider the blood of Jesus as the best antidote to the poison-infested life. Personally, I had tried all of the alternatives and found the cross and the blood of Jesus to be more than adequate.

However, Carol's counselor not only referred her to another worldly professional who administered a controlled substance known as anti-depressants . . . but also hooked her up with a clique known as a support group. Within this support group were individuals who were going through similar trials. Their code of secrecy allowed them to dwell on the past in the name of therapy. Along with the swapping of stories and situations, their code of secrecy also enabled them to swap their pills. More than a battered woman, Carol found herself at the foot of the cross (three years after her first visit to this counselor) as a drug addict, divorced, repetitiously digging up her past, and still trying to deal with her sins, an ex-husband, and a whole pile of guilt.

Carol continued to remain loyal to her counselor and a so-called friend who had "adopted" Carol as her daughter. This friend, referred by Carol's counselor, took on the title of mentor. After a while, the mentor/friend told Carol to refer to her as Mom. There was a substantial age difference between Carol and her much older mentor, now known as "Mom". Carol's mentor swapped friendship for pills. Numerous times the mentor went into Carol's apartment, without telling Carol, in order to obtain the controlled substance known as anti-depressants. When the mentor's supply ran out, and Carol's supply had been depleted, the game plan shifted to insurance fraud. Carol's mentor taught Carol how to get pills through her medical insurance. With a supply that didn't require money, Carol's mentor continued to assure her that it was OK because the need was so great.

Carol's status as a single mom and full-time worker had limited her to almost no personal life outside the clique known as a support group. In spite of her addiction and present situation, she managed to make it to her church picnic on a sunny Sunday afternoon. It was ironic that I was playing first base and she assumed the position of right field during the co-ed baseball game. As each inning ended, Carol would jog by me—and at one point, between innings, Carol and I started talking. Our conversation on the baseball field moved up to lengthy phone conversations. I'll spare most of those details lest this turn into a romantic novel. Somehow I think you get the picture. We went from three hour phone conversations to a date, then two dates, and so on. Somewhere in about our second month of dating, Carol was confronted by her counselor and mentor. They informed Carol that I was "Bad News". Carol didn't tell me about the confrontation until weeks later. Both of our ex-spouses were remarried and Carol and I were very much in love. We decided to get married. Within a few weeks of our marriage, Carol's counselor and several opinionated followers left the church.

Through the love of Jesus, Carol weaned herself off the pills and increased her Bible study and trust in the Lord. Carol had read my first book, *A Garment of Grace*, and figured if Jesus could do it for her new husband just a few years earlier, He could do it for her now. And that He did. I'm here to tell you it was no cake walk and I'll not get into the specifics of Carol's withdrawal from the anti-depressants. But for the mercy and grace of God through Carol's faith in Jesus Christ, I got me a drug-free spouse who is on fire for the Lord.

I didn't take the deceptive warnings Carol received about me from her counselor and mentor personally. Both Carol and I realize that it wasn't me that bothered them but it was what I stood for. We also realized that sheep don't eat other sheep and if you have a problem with another Christian, talking behind their back is never an option. Matthew, chapter 18, verses 15—17 reads: "If your brother sins against you, go and show him his fault, just between the two of you. If he listens to you, you have won your brother over. But if he will not listen, take one or two others along, so that 'every matter may be established by the testimony of two or three witnesses.' If he refuses to listen to them, tell it to the church; and if he refuses to listen even to the church, treat him as you would a pagan or a tax collector."

Part III: The Wool Over My Eyes

The pastor was teaching a series titled *What Ever Happened to Common Sense?* He opened the series with this statement: "There are three ways a person can obtain common sense. They are either born with it, they can borrow it, or they can have it beat into them." It was also stressed that a person could lose their common sense if their focus became clouded by the world and its standards. Like sheep, sometimes our exteriors can become thick and we need a good shearing. If you have ever seen sheep after the wool has been sheared, well, they look gangly and pitiful as they try to adjust to the environment without their thick exteriors. Sheep become accustomed to the thick coat and I believe they feel more secure with it. It's kind of like me when I was a boy. I would hide underneath the covers in my bed. My blankets were monster-proof, bullet-proof, and were also able to protect me from anything I didn't want to deal with that mentally I had sold myself out to.

Most of the counsel Carol and I had received over the years had created a false sense of security. Problem areas of our lives that God defines as sin had been misrepresented by worldly professionals. Characteristics that God had intended for one purpose had been trimmed in an un-Christlike fashion. Some of the trimming left irreversible results and deep scars. It's devastating to think about having a wolf loose in your flock with a pair of razor-sharp shears. Manicuring a sheep's exterior so the wool ends up blocking its hindsight as well as its foresight is a common practice in today's counseling arena. The same clippers that are useful for shearing . . . in the wrong hands can be used to literally fillet an innocent lamb. Especially when the clippers end up in paws that belong to a wolf. Matthew, chapter 7, verses 15—20 reads like this: "Watch out for false prophets. They come to you in sheep's clothing, but inwardly they are ferocious wolves. By their fruit you will recognize them. Do people pick grapes from thornbushes, or figs from thistles? Likewise every good tree bears good fruit, but a bad tree bears bad fruit. A good tree cannot bear bad fruit, and a bad tree cannot bear good fruit. Every tree that does not bear good fruit is cut down and thrown into the fire. Thus, by their fruit you will recognize them."

᷾᷾ ᷾᷾ ᷾᷾ ᷾᷾ ᷾᷾

Whatever happened to common sense? That's a good question. If you're like Carol and myself and had it beat into you, you're likely to learn to appreciate a faithful Savior named Jesus Christ, the Word of God which is the Bible, Christian service that has become Servanthood, the support of a congregation and loyal believers defined as Fellowship, and the commitment of a shepherd known as the Pastor.

The Execution Of A Man

Today I witnessed the execution of a man. I saw one man destroyed by another man. I watched as his life diminished before my very eyes. The trap-door opened. The man dropped. With a horrendous jerk, at the end of a long rope, twitching muscles were all that was left of a once life-filled body . . . He fought for oxygen as the chemical gas filled his lungs and within seconds he sat there with a lifeless stare . . . His body wretched and struggled in an effort to overcome the lethally injected serum that flowed from the point of entry into a beating muscle known as the heart . . . His body jerked in several directions as the bullets pounded through his chest cavity. In his final agonizing moments he cries out, "Why Me? Why Me?"

Today I witnessed the execution of a man. I listened as one man destroyed another man. I was a fool to pay tribute to another man's grudge. His bitterness became a reality in my mind. Today I listened to a man become a judge, a jury, and an executioner. I became the rope in a verbal hanging of another human being. I was the carrier as I breathed the poison gas into another's ear. The thoughts have become a part of me and manifested themselves in my heart like the poison injected and bent on destruction. The bullets of deceit are aimed directly at his integrity, credibility, self esteem, and good reputation.

In our homes, it's an ungodly heritage we pass on to our children. In our circle of friends, it's a means of gaining popularity. In our church, it's the accusation against a pastor, elder, or deacon. In the work place, it's a way of proving ourselves more qualified for the position. In politics, it's a strategic move for men to rise to the top.

After watching his older brother tortured, mutilated, and executed both verbally and physically, an author known as James wrote these words some forty-four years after the tragedy: "Who is wise and understanding among you? Let him show it by his good life, by deeds done in humility that comes from wisdom. But if you harbor bitter envy and selfish ambition in your hearts, do not boast about it or deny the truth. Such 'wisdom' does not come down from heaven but is earthly, unspiritual, of the devil. For where you have envy and selfish ambition, there you find disorder and every evil practice. But the wisdom that comes from heaven is first of all pure; then peace-loving, considerate, submissive, full of mercy and good fruit, impartial and sincere. Peacemakers who sow in peace raise a harvest of righteousness."

Today I witnessed the execution of a man and he cried out, "Why Me? Why Me?" Yes, I listened as one man destroyed another.

2a 2a 2a 2a 2a

Earl was pleasant and his personality remarkably kind. I would have to say he was probably one of the most kind-hearted men I've ever known. His smile spoke clearly of the personal relationship he had with Christ. Earl sold insurance and would frequently stop in at the motorhome and recreational vehicle dealership that I worked for. He was persistent but tactful in his efforts to get referrals to add to his new customer list. Earl intrigued me with his honesty and solid business practices. I shared with him the success that I had been having selling motorhomes. I was the assistant sales manager at this dealership, and being the top man was a desire that lingered in my mind, but my reliability had been more than hindered by my periodic alcohol and cocaine abuse. The owner of the motorhome and R.V. dealership also owned two other franchises. He had followed in his father's footsteps and ended up with a new car dealership that he expanded and built up to a multi-franchised business that had several locations. The owner had shared openly with me that he had been a prisoner to alcohol for a number of years. His victory over his drinking had given him a tremendous insight into others with similar sins. At any rate, he had my number and had fired me numerous times only to hire me back. The owner's forgiving, understanding, and empathetic attitude is still an unforgotten memory. The Lord seems to recall his second and third chances every time I start to get even a little impatient with someone else.

There are some sins that are repairable with time and others we have to live with until death do us part. There is one memory, however, that keeps popping up and will continue to do so as long as I'm on this side of eternity. I suppose it's because the memory is the by-product of one of the number one killers of all humanity. At the very least it is responsible for 50% of all hurts and hardships. The tape of this memory plays over and over in my mind as I witness its uncontrollable, destructive force being lived out in the lives of others. The irrefutable characteristic of this hideous sinful act can be recognized by me because "*It takes one to know one*".

It was a real blow to my ego when I found myself playing second tune to Earl when he became the new sales manager. In my mind, I was more qualified for the position. I had more product knowledge than Earl did and I had been in the business years longer. I had given the sales records a new name for numbers. I was respected for these results but no one knew the bitter envy I carried inside towards Earl. The more qualified I thought myself to be than Earl, the more bitter my heart became. I made myself a victim in my own mind to justify my actions of deceit. If anyone had told me that I lacked the qualifications of humility, honesty, reliability, and integrity that it took to be a leader, I would have only found myself shifting the blame. The plain and simple fact is that I was a jealous and rotten person inside and my alcohol and drug abuse were only results of massive insecurity and the old scheme of tearing others down to build oneself up. Whether in word, deed, or both—it became a mindset and a way of life that, if not for a bath in the blood of Christ, would have literally killed me. I'm not sure who wrote this, but I'll quote it as well as I can remember: "Alcohol and drugs are coping devices for an underlying problem. Failure to deal with the underlying problem is failure to deal with alcohol and drug abuse. The answer to each of the above is Jesus Christ."

In Earl's last days at the dealership, his countenance looked drained . . . he was a tired and worn out man ready to give up. His speech and attitude never reflected anger or retaliation toward his accusers. His eyes were stained with the tears of a hopeless situation, yet within them there still burned the light of eternity.

I don't carry the guilt around anymore for what I did to Earl, but I do carry the memory. I have since come to realize that I crucified another man a few thousand years ago who reacted pretty much the same way.

The Beam and Speck Syndrome

It had been eight years since I grew my last beard. I've watched the brown hair on the top of my head give way to a lighter color called grey. In fact, some of the hair on my head has just plain given way.

Curious to see what the years had done to the hair on my chin, cheeks, and neck, I decided to face a new look each morning. My wife's complaining about my looks and her quick, to the point kisses let me know that she wasn't nearly as curious as I was about the color of the prickly follicles that began to protrude from my face.

About six months ago, I had to accept what my friends called "The Big Four-O". Forty years old brought some new looks and the hairy addition to my chin, cheeks, and neck was indeed more grey than anything else. In answer to one of my bald church friends who made a joking remark about my scruffy beard, I replied that I had grown it for him. He looked puzzled because I sounded serious. I went on to tell him that I'd heard he was going to have a hair transplant and I had graciously grown my beard just for him so that I could be the donor.

Taking a look at ourselves can become very overwhelming. Sometimes it's extremely difficult to take ourselves at "face value". We seem to develop this subtle concept of, "that can't be me! I would never do or say that!" We achieve acceptance in our jobs and ministries, and perhaps are respected in most circles. However, deep inside us there lingers this sort of evil that we know is there. Our sin nature begins to protrude in our attitudes and manifests itself in our outlook on our fellow man. In the church arena, or as members of God's family, we at times get this sort of inner pride that makes statements to others. Statements that with our attitudes say, "We've Arrived." It seems at times this attitude, when manifested in its extremes, will look at salvation as being earned rather than as a gift that could never be bought short of a miracle. We walk with Jesus and share fellowship with other believers; yet when put to the test, we fail. The plain and ugly truth is: we see ourselves as being better than others. Seeing ourselves as better than others in and of itself is un-Christlike. We bear the title of Christian and yet somehow, in our complacency, we feel as if we've become immune to sin. Unfortunately, we've missed one of the most important Christlike attributes of being saved. From the moment we ask Jesus into our hearts, we should start dying to self. The walk, the talk, and the service are just the outward reflections of the inward commitment of dying to self. The true motives of a person will be exposed if all their years of service are a self- service, lacking in the Christlikeness of dying to self. The end result of this scenario is usually the slinging of insults.

A very prominent pastor had received a proposal from a television station. The television station wanted to do a documentary on the pastor, the church, and the massive growth in numbers the congregation had experienced over the past few years.

The first day of filming, a middle-aged cameraman was specifically assigned to the pastor. The cameraman's job also consisted of being an associate producer, so he was to take the words and the narrative content of the documentary and illustrate them within the video portion of the film.

The preacher was a boisterous sort of man with a tremendous sense of humor. His attitude of godliness always seemed to manifest itself in some of the most unique situations. Today was no different. As the middle-aged cameraman set his camera pod up in the middle of the sanctuary, he began his normal routine of focusing and getting the proper lighting through the iris. The iris was part of the huge intricate lens that protruded from the front of the camera. The preacher looked at the T.V. monitor which sat a few feet off to the side of the camera.

As the camera scanned the sanctuary and brought into view the empty pews, the cameraman looked over at the preacher and stated in a somewhat monotone voice, "It's kind of spooky in here without all the people." The pastor tipped his head to the side, peered over the top of his glasses, and gave a sort of inquisitive look. The cameraman went on to tell the pastor, "You know, the last time I was in church was 30 years ago. I just couldn't handle all the hypocrites. There were more fights and feuds over the pettiest things. I lost my wife and family right in the middle of all that turmoil to a social disease called divorce. The people in the congregation were more concerned with their own little petty things. They still had their families together and at a time when I really needed them, they just weren't there."

The pastor remained silent and the cameraman's voice became a little louder, "And if that wasn't enough, the church ended up in a split and I was a loser no matter which side I took. I knew of numerous affairs that were going on within the membership. I was also a Sunday school teacher and some of the church leadership ridiculed me because of the content of my lessons. I just couldn't take no more!" The cameraman's voice subsided and the pastor looked at him and stated, "I know what you mean!"

The pastor asked the cameraman to step aside and the pastor assumed the position behind the camera. The pastor told the cameraman to keep his eyes on the monitor and as the pastor swung the camera around, a picture appeared on the screen. The pastor mimicked the cameraman, turned a couple of lenses, and the out of focus image became as clear as could be. The image on the monitor was a picture of Christ that hung on the back wall of the sanctuary.

After a moment of silence, the pastor looked over at the cameraman and stated, "We have a song we sing in our Sunday school department. The words to the song go something like this:

> 'O, be careful little eyes what you see.
> O, be careful little eyes what you see.
> 'Cause the father up above
> is looking down with love.
> So, be careful little eyes what you see.
> O, be careful little ears what you hear.
> O, be careful little ears what you hear.
> 'Cause the father up above
> is looking down with love.
> So, be careful little ears what you hear.
> O, be careful little mouth what you speak.
> O, be careful little mouth what you speak.
> 'Cause the father up above
> is looking down with love.
> So, be careful little mouth what you speak.'"

Before the cameraman could respond, the pastor continued, "You see, Mr. Cameraman, your head and mind are a lot like this camera. The images you see and the words you hear are recorded and in turn are expressed with your mouth and your attitude. The images, the words, and the attitude you express; you express by choice. It all depends on the direction you're pointed. All those images you see, words you hear, and things you say find their way to your heart, just like that monitor over there. Your heart projects whatever your mind is pointed at.

For the past years, Mr. Cameraman, your problem hasn't been other people, it's been you. If you'll show up for church this Sunday, perhaps we can start to get your camera pointed in the right direction. And if you'll read your Bible, pray, and show up for other activities and really become involved in the building up of God's family, rather than the tearing down of it, perhaps this image you see over here will become more in focus."

     ❧ ❧ ❧ ❧ ❧

Let's remember once again the two criminals who hung next to Christ. One criminal died two deaths while the other only one death. The criminal who refused the dying to self hurled insults at the Son of God. This poor criminal was consumed with his dilemma of death and his overwhelming surroundings. Thus the challenge was put to God to remove the circumstances rather than to accept them. This criminal became a legacy in the age-old art of refusing to die to self. I recall an elderly man of about eighty-five years old telling me that dying to self is a daily struggle. He also told me that perfection of this spirit-filled attribute of dying to self will be made complete with the physical death for all who know Christ as Lord and Savior.

Refusing to take on the Savior's characteristics in every aspect of our lives is the biggest insult to our Lord, not to mention the hinderance to the testimony of the born again believer in Jesus Christ.

If one criminal could look at the Son of God and try to find a spot, while the other looked at Christ as Savior and speckless . . . it's pretty easy to conclude that there are no grey areas. Either we accept our sins and see a savior or we hurl insults and shift the blame.

Until we accept ourselves at face value, for who we are and not what we *think* we are, we will continue to victimize ourselves with the age-old nature of the Beam and Speck Syndrome. Jesus addressed this Beam and Speck Syndrome in

Matthew, chapter 7, verses 3—5. It reads like this: "Why do you look at the speck of sawdust in your brother's eye and pay no attention to the plank in your own eye? How can you say to your brother, 'Let me take the speck out of your eye,' when all the time there is a plank in your own eye? You hypocrite, first take the plank out of your own eye, and then you will see clearly to remove the speck from your brother's eye."

Addressed to the religious people of Jesus' day, our Savior carried this message all the way to Calvary and allowed it to be exhibited by a criminal who hung directly next to Him. Moments before his death and at a time when this criminal really needed a savior, he turned down his only hope for salvation by refusing Christ with an attitude that was anything but a self-examination. This criminal died physically from an execution. He was never able to live spiritually and eternally for God because of his self-inflicted Beam and Speck Syndrome. This criminal carried this Beam and Speck Syndrome from the cross through the gates of eternal damnation where he'll serve an eternity of weeping and the gnashing of teeth. His cries of agony are echoed through the very depths of hell and are heard by all those who have embarked on the same path.

CHAPTER 16

Count The Sunny Days

I was told, what seems like a long time ago, that my lack of acceptance had almost destroyed me physically, emotionally, and spiritually. Running a close second to my lack of acceptance was my inability to be patient. This human stupidity had plagued my life for years. I was gung-ho for Jesus and prayed earnestly for patience and acceptance. There is nothing wrong with being gung-ho for Jesus. However, when you earnestly pray for patience and acceptance, well, I'll tell you; if you must, ask for them one at a time—and at least two years apart.

I didn't know, when I started my associate pastoral work in a Christian retirement home, that acceptance would be the key to survival. I think it was my first day there when one of the older staff members told me to hold my hands out with my palms up. The question was asked, "Do you see any nail scars, Dennis?" I replied with, "No!" At which the staff member reported, "You're not a savior!" I wanted to retaliate with, "Then what am I doing here?" But I decided to exercise my godly character and keep my tongue still.

I wanted to minister to the elderly and share Jesus with them. I had my plan of action in order and possessed all of the appropriate scriptures to deal with pain and suffering.

I found myself in the chaplain's office, at the end of my first day, frustrated inside and tears running down my cheeks.

Everything I had prepared from scripture was true but out of context. There were amputees, cancer and stroke victims, and Alzheimer's disease patients. It seemed each one of the residents had lost, or were losing, their ability to live. I wanted to change them, and their situations, to a Happily-Ever-After. I believe the senior chaplain, whom I was pastoring under, knew what was happening inside me. I tried not to let on to the anguish I was feeling and I never told him how devastated I was. I think he knew. I'm sure he knew. After a few days, I found myself letting go of my plans. Little by little, as time passed, I began adapting to, and living in, God's design for the residents instead of mine. Second Corinthians, chapter 1, verse 9 reads like this: "Indeed, in our hearts we felt the sentence of death. But this happened that we might not rely on ourselves but on God, who raises the dead."

God was showing me His way. The Holy Spirit began teaching and training me in the Christlike art of acceptance. God had placed me in the perfect environment to grant my prayer request; the request for acceptance. Those of you who have mastered the art of acceptance know that patience is interwoven with acceptance. You're probably at least 70 years old too! When a child of God learns acceptance, he or she must learn perseverance to see a situation through to the end. Somewhere in all of this we find the Holy Spirit giving birth to patience. Colossians, chapter 1, verses 11 and 12 reads like this: "Being strengthened with all power according to His glorious might so that you may have great endurance and patience, and joyfully giving thanks to the Father, who has qualified you to share in the inheritance of the saints in the kingdom of light."

Each new challenge that arose from my friends, who resided in this home for the aged, reflected in my performance a little saying my mother had on her refrigerator door. It went something like this: "*I finally got it all together, but I forgot where I put it.*" That's right! Each new endeavor for ministry to the elderly showed me that patience begins with a strong relationship with the Savior. Patience is something that grows in someone through suffering, trials, and sometimes just plain giving up on oneself. Patience is the essence of a peaceful walk with Jesus, and realizing that He is in absolute control.

One might ask, "Okay Dennis, what makes you such an expert?" I'm not! Believe me! However, in the environment that God had placed me in, my Lord introduced me to one of the residents who would express acceptance, perseverance, patience, and an overwhelming commitment to Jesus Christ; a commitment that had been so strong for so long that even in her present condition her faithfulness to Jesus left her still praising and sharing her Lord with me; a commitment that was made from an unconditional love for Christ.

Ethel was clinically described as being stroke paralyzed. Her body, all but one arm, had been immobilized due to brain hemorrhaging. She was lifted and strapped to a wheelchair when she went to chapel. Most of her time was spent laying down with a slight incline to her bed. She could hear, see, talk, and express herself, and her Lord, well. Her speech had almost no emphasis on words—but the love of Christ, and the content of those words describing her love for her Lord, penetrated my heart with pleasant and overwhelming feelings of love, joy, peace, patience, kindness, goodness, faithfulness, gentleness, and self-control. Ethel's heart was a *Horn Of Plenty*, filled with all the fruit of the Spirit.

In a monotone voice, she would thank me for my help. I started spending more and more time with Ethel. I began remembering my prayer to the Lord asking Him to give me patience and acceptance. I listened to my friend describe a diary one of her girl friends had given her on her 21st birthday some 60 years ago. On the front of the diary were the words *"Count The Sunny Days"*. Ethel told me she kept the diary current for many years and that she never wrote anything bad in it. This beautiful person told me, "When I am awake, I pray and thank my Jesus for my life. And when I'm asleep, He sends me dreams; nice pleasant dreams about my family. All the good memories and fun times are like movies. My Lord plays them over and over for me. I never have a bad dream."

I began to realize that God was answering my prayer request. Ethel was ministering to me. Ethel was able to minister to me because I began to see her the way my Lord saw blind men, lepers, prostitutes, and tax collectors. Jesus looked through the sin, the sickness, and the hopelessness that the critics and religious leaders would see—and He saw the real opportunity for ministry; the ministry of humility and compassion; a ministry of serving needs and glorifying His Heavenly Father. Christ looked at Himself as being less than those He ministered to. He humbled Himself to serve people.

Jesus, knowing what was ahead of Him, was able to accept the cross, because He considered Ethel, myself, and all mankind's need for salvation to be greater than His right to be God. Jesus accepted, and persevered patiently, the torture and suffering of Roman crucifixion because He trusted His Heavenly Father to reveal Himself and His plan. What normal men saw as a tragedy, Jesus saw as an opportunity to save all mankind from eternal damnation. Ethel saw her condition as an opportunity to glorify her Lord.

The key to acceptance and patience is: "Esteeming others as being greater than oneself". It's called "Christlike humility". That type of character is not always easy to portray, but it's a far better life than any of the options—and it's much more rewarding spiritually.

Ethel's diary, with *"Count The Sunny Days"* written on the front, holds a special thought in my heart. When my focus begins to drift and I find myself trying to change the unchangeable, or speed up the divine process, I remember the humility Christ showed for me at Calvary. I ponder how He reflected that character in a lovely old lady, who was paralyzed in body but not in spirit, and I count my blessings.

One of those blessings is an eternal blessing. It's recorded in a book in heaven with Ethel's name and my name inside. There isn't anything bad in this book either. Thanks to Jesus, Ethel and I will be able to *"Count The Sunny Days"* for eternity.

CHAPTER 17

A Mother's Day Promise
From the Cross

I have heard people call her know-it-all, outspoken, opinionated, Bible thumper, and even Christian. I believe the
most blasphemous expression I ever heard spoken of her
was the word co-dependent. I was one of three. Many
thought I was her favorite. I don't believe so. I was just the
most disrespectful, rebellious, and disappointing. I know she
lived in the hope that someday Christ would own all of me.
When my dad was killed, I was six years old. I had a brother
a year younger and a sister a year older. In later years, I would
become the middleman. I would be the person that would
cause her to be a prayer warrior. Her most favorite? Not at
all! I was just 1/3 of her responsibility requiring 70% of her
time and getting 80% of the grace. At age 37, I entered seminary. I left behind a prison record. Through my reckless
ways, I had lost all of my family but her. The past tragedies
were too numerous to count. By the time Christ had all of
me, no one else wanted anything to do with me. Popular
opinion was to condemn me.

Two thousand years ago, at the foot of a cross, another
mother stood by her son when popular opinion was to crucify
Him. She watched her son tortured beyond anything man had
ever seen or ever would see. His pain-stricken and mutilated

149

body hung on a cross exposed to, and in redemption for, everything I had ever done or would do. My Lord's love for His mother, and her godly character towards her son would be passed on in His Word to my mother. She never gave up her hope for me. She never quit praying for me. A few years ago, I entered the ministry as a published author and speaker. From time to time, in her heart, my mom still hears the Savior's reply: *"Woman, Behold Thy Son!"*